STANDING
AT THE EDGE OF
GREATNESS

SHELLEY BERAD

urbanpress

Standing at the Edge of Greatness
by Shelley Berad
Copyright © 2018 Shelley Berad

ISBN # 978-1-63360-083-6

For Worldwide Distribution   Printed in the U.S.A.

Urban Press
P.O. Box 8881
Pittsburgh, PA 15221-0881 USA
412.646.2780
www.urbanpress.us

May you be encouraged by the words of this book.

Shelley Berad

Contents

Preface

When I was a child and just learning to read, my Grandmother Ruth started writing letters to me. I was barely old enough to string a few sentences together in reply, but this began a decades-long correspondence between us through mailed letters, many of which I still have and cherish today. In many ways, this fostered my love of writing and taught me how to express myself concerning the things God was laying on my heart and teaching me. Her most important and consistent message to me was to know that God loved me, and that I was special to Him. Whenever I visited her, she regularly asked me what I was doing to serve God, how I was using my time and talents for Him, and what I had been reading in my devotions. I knew when I went to visit Grandmom that I better have answers ready for her.

Faith was as much a part of my grandmother's life as was breathing. She would sing old hymns to me when she rocked me in her rocking chair, and would pray for me every single day. The joy of the Lord was truly her strength.

As I grew older, I began to send many letters of my own to friends, family, and to anyone whom God placed on my heart. While the medium has changed and many people now write emails and texts instead of letters, I still choose to correspond with handwritten cards whenever possible, just as my grandmother did. The written word is still powerful in our age of technology. It has a way of grabbing hold of our attention like no other form of communication can. The more I wrote over the years, the more I realized that it was a gift God had given me, and He wanted me to take it seriously and use it for His glory.

When I began writing a blog in 2007, it was almost always about my children describing simple but entertaining stories of my initial plunge into parenting. As the years progressed and life took some rather unexpected and difficult turns, my blog entries became much more than family anecdotes. They were therapeutic to me and a lifeline to others, a chance to share my deepest emotions and the ways God was teaching me in the midst of some very deep valleys.

I am frequently asked if I always planned to have a large family. My answer is always a resounding no. Something changed in my heart, however, as I began to raise my children. Something in me was touched in a way I never had been touched before. Each and every day, in significant or small ways, my children have taught me lessons. Much of my inspiration, hope, and strength are derived from the way God points things out to me through my children.

I see in them such a vivid picture of the ways I relate to Him. It is both humbling and thought-provoking. It has profoundly changed me in ways I never could have imagined. With their own unique challenges and personalities, each child has enabled me to view the world around me through a different set of lenses. My oldest, Carter, is ten; next is my daughter Reese who is eight; Sienna is five; Lawson is three; and Evangeline is one. God's plan for my family and me was much larger than mine ever was.

He knew exactly what I would need and when I would need it. In the midst of everything I have experienced in my life in the past several years, He's given me these beautiful children to care for. Many days when I didn't have the desire or strength to go on, they gave me that extra push to keep going. I had to get up and keep parenting them, keep taking care of them. As I did that while grieving, God brought healing to my heart. Through them, He often showed me startling and humbling snapshots of my relationship with Him.

I started writing because I was drowning in sorrow and He rescued me. I was going down a path of destruction and He showed me a better way. He is using this stage of my life, the sacred vocation of parenting, to put a visual image in my mind, one of His own love for me. When my heart wells up for my little ones, I'm ever more aware of His love for me. His love, the intensity of it, often catches me off guard. It surprises and delights me, and I'm forever grateful. I want to share what I have learned with others and that is part of the reason for this book. We are all standing on the edge of greatness, but sometimes the fog of circumstances can cloud our perspective.

My grandmother passed away in late 2013 and I miss the covering of her prayers and her calming presence in my life. Over the last four years, I've lost a friend, my siblings, am losing a parent, and much more. In many ways, I felt the life I once had was completely stripped away from me. There were moments I wanted to throw up my hands in defeat, but God had much bigger plans for me. When He pressed on my heart the idea of publishing a book with the things I had written during these difficulties, I cried out, "Right now, God? How will I ever be able to do a thing like that while raising five young children and in so much pain?" Again and again, God made it clear to me that this was the time.

I credit this entire book to God and to the daily inspirations He has given me. I pray they are an encouragement to you and a light shining into your own dark places. May you find strength in Him to go on, when you think you can't take one more step forward, and may you consider a relationship with Him if you never have before.

> But me he caught—reached all the way from sky to sea; he pulled me out of that ocean of hate, that enemy chaos, the void in which I was drowning. They hit me when I was down, but God stuck by me. He stood me up on a wide-open field; I stood there saved—surprised to be loved! (Psalm 18:16-19 MSG)

Shelley Berad
Pittsburgh, PA
April 2018

Introduction

I've been to Ground Zero, both physically and emotionally. A few months after the 9/11 attacks on New York City, I visited the former site of the World Trade Center Towers. I stood at a fence which surrounded a vast pit of rubble; earth movers were everywhere cleaning up and relocating the debris. Many buildings were still standing with gaping holes in them. In the midst of this wasteland of what once was, I noticed metal beams in the shape of a cross pulled from the wreckage, and standing on a pedestal in the center of the destruction. It took my breath away when I first saw it because it was so unexpected. In that place of desolation and despair, it was a stark reminder to me of God's presence in the midst of tragedy.

Thirteen years later, I found myself in another place of personal desolation when a single phone call rocked my world. That call informed me that a friend of many years had taken the lives of two of her own children. I sobbed, not believing something like this could truly occur. My heart ached for her devastated family, and for her. For an entire year, a small gift bag sat tucked away in a corner of my bedroom closet – a gift that had never been and could never be given. The gift was for one of those children. How God, how could something this horrific happen? Surely I would never experience anything else so tragically sad in my life! Guilt, sorrow, regret, and despair racked my spirit and brought me before the Lord again and again in tears. The question rang out in my mind repeatedly like a broken record: "Why?" Slowly my heart experienced healing. Life, though forever changed, began to return to "normal."

Then in January of 2015, I found out that my younger brother Ed would be visiting my parents in New Jersey for a weekend. It was a difficult time to travel with my four young kids, one just a few months old. I initially told my mom that we wouldn't be coming out this time, but would wait to see Ed the next time he came out for a visit. Something kept tugging at me and prompting me, however, to make that trip, and at the last minute we decided to go.

We only saw Ed for one day. He was there to pack all his remaining belongings that were still in the U.S. and have them shipped to his future home in Thailand. It was a surreal time, saying goodbye to my brother as he made a move to the other side of the world where his wife was from. We were excited for him, however, and for this new chapter of his life, which he'd been working toward for years. A moving truck showed up and packed all his things. He signed off on some papers and that was the end. Everything from his childhood room was gone. I remember standing in the room where the starkness of it impacted me; there was nothing left.

Ed played with my children, letting them drag one of his rock climbing ropes all throughout the house like a giant snake. He had such a natural ability to relate to and have fun with them. Before we left, I snapped a couple of photos of Ed, standing in front of my childhood home with both of my parents. It was hard for me to imagine how life would change so dramatically from that point, and I never could have imagined the events that would play out in the next few months.

The last time I heard from Ed was in April of 2015 when a postcard came in the mail. He sent it from a recent trip he had been on in Asia, saying he missed me and couldn't wait to come and visit us again soon.

I sat in a dimly-lit room, rocking eight-month-old Lawson to sleep on the evening of May 24, 2015. The next day was Memorial Day, and as I sat, I recalled a tradition we once had as children. We would decorate our bikes with red, white and blue crepe paper and bike into town for a Memorial Day parade.

Still rocking my son, my thoughts of those happy times shifted to another memory. Growing up, we lived along a busy road. A distressed man rang our doorbell while we were eating dinner one evening. He had struck a biker with his vehicle right in front of our house and killed him. I was shaken remembering this and how we never biked on that road again after that. And in an inexplicable way, I felt prompted to send both my siblings an email letting them know that I loved them.

The next day, Memorial Day, I went to a parade with my kids, played with them in the sunshine all day, and fell into bed exhausted at midnight. One hour later, I was awakened to receive the worst news of my young life. My brother Ed had lost his footing while rock climbing at a great height, and had plummeted to his death when his wall anchors dislodged and failed to break his fall.

For two weeks, we waited to have his funeral, since there was a police investigation that had to be conducted prior to releasing his body. I spent my evenings, after the kids went to bed, writing a eulogy for his funeral. One day while at the grocery store, the clerk at the register smiled and asked, "How are you today?" Of course, I gave her the pat, "I'm fine, how are you?" but "fine" could not have been further from the truth.

I never got to say goodbye and it still haunts me to this day. There were so many things I would have told him – how much I loved and appreciated him, and what an amazing, thoughtful, and caring brother he was, just to name a few. I would never have a chance to say those things along with many other expressions of love that I found in my heart. Everywhere I looked in my house there were items from all over the world that he lovingly found and gave me and my kids, trinkets and treasures from his worldwide adventures. My throat tightened for the thousandth time as I remembered all the times we spent together and how it was all cut short far too soon.

I returned to my hometown in New Jersey for my "little" brother's funeral in June of 2015. How could he be gone at age 31? I felt as if I was having an out-of-body experience. Was this really happening, God? How could it possibly be that Ed is gone?

I stood up in front of a room packed with friends and family to give a eulogy that I'd spent the previous two weeks preparing. It didn't even feel as if I was the one speaking. People looked at me, wondering what I could possibly say at a time like this.

One of the passages I shared that day was from 2 Corinthians 12:9-10:

> But he said to me, "My grace is sufficient for you, for my power is made perfect in weakness." Therefore I will boast all the more gladly about my weaknesses, so that Christ's power may rest on me. That is why, for Christ's sake, I delight in weaknesses, in insults, in hardships, in persecutions, in difficulties. For when I am weak, then I am strong.

I didn't feel strong at all. I felt like my entire world was crumbling around me, and that was just the beginning. After the funeral, we went back to my parents' house to meet with our friends and family. Many people offered words of kindness, promises of prayer, and hugs to soothe my broken heart. My parents had been preparing for a move to Pittsburgh for months, so the house was empty of all contents that day, except for the essentials. Their move date was only a few weeks away, and this was not at all the way they expected to say goodbye to their home and state where they'd spent many decades living their lives and raising a family.

My sister-in-law had only been married to Ed for about two years and soon it was time for her to return to Thailand. I could not imagine the trauma and overwhelming ache in her heart after so many hopes and dreams were shattered in an instant by a sudden fall. As she and her family said goodbye and pulled out of the driveway, I turned to my mom and my aunt who were standing next to me and burst into tears. I wondered then if I would ever see her again after she traveled back to Thailand to pick up the pieces of her broken life. What would ever bring us together again?

The following day I packed up my own family to leave. I walked around the house, slowly and methodically. I looked in every room, pausing to reminisce. Everywhere I looked, I retrieved many wonderful, happy memories of a time when things were much more carefree. I walked around the yard where I had spent many hours playing with my brothers as a child. In a few weeks, that house would not be a part of my family any longer.

I stopped on my way down the front walkway. There in the cement, weathered and faint with the passage of time, was a set of tiny footprints and some writing, "Shelley – 1980." I'd been born and raised there, and saying goodbye to my home was harder than I ever imagined. As we departed to return to Pittsburgh, driving down roads I'd traveled countless times, I sobbed. It was a time I thought would be joyful, a time when my parents would finally be moving to be close to my family. Right then, however, all I felt was sorrow.

A few weeks later, my parents made the move to Pittsburgh in July of 2015. It was good to have them near and to see them anytime I wanted. What had once been a six-hour drive to visit them now required two minutes. We were grieving deeply, trying to make sense of all that had happened and to find hope for the days ahead. As I carefully observed my mom, however, I noticed that she seemed different. She was getting confused, forgetting more and more.

When her cat ran away just after the move, Mom placed some big poster boards in her front yard that read, "Lost Cat." Taped to the back of those posters were pictures of my brother from birth to adulthood, which had been on display at his viewing. As I pulled into my parent's driveway that day, I noticed some of the priceless photos blowing across the yard. I stooped to pick them up, pressing them to my heart, and the weight of it all hit me like a wrecking ball. *How had my world been torn apart like this in a matter of weeks?*

Weeks passed and Mom continued to struggle. I wasn't ready to admit just yet that this was more than grief. It couldn't be anything worse, or so I hoped. I was not strong enough to handle another loss on the heels of losing my brother. Nevertheless, just weeks after my brother's funeral, I was forced to come to terms with the devastating news that I was losing my mom to a debilitating and incurable illness.

It was September of 2015 when I received an email from my sister-in-law, my brother's widow. It was a short and rather cryptic message and she just said that she had some good news she wanted to share with my parents and me. I hadn't done a good job staying in touch with her up till then, but looked forward to catching up when she called. We set up a time for the video chat and as the three of us sat at the computer, waiting for her face to appear on the screen, I wondered what she might have to tell us.

Suddenly, my life seemed to stand still yet again as she shared with us that she was 20-weeks pregnant. My brother and she had found out they were expecting their first child, just three days before his death. In a moment that should have been pure joy, I was overcome with sorrow. Ed should have been there next to her sharing this news with us. He should have seen our smiles and heard our excitement. Of course, we were stunned and overjoyed that this miracle baby was now a part of our lives, a beacon of hope amidst our storm. We congratulated my sister-in-law, told her how much we loved her, and our call ended.

After that, the what-ifs haunted me more and more. The agony of what could have been ate at my resolve, courage, and heart. More than anything, I wished I lived closer to my sister-in-law so I could at least offer her comfort and support, but she was living with her parents in Thailand, and that was the best place she could have been. The baby would arrive in January. We marked the due date on our calendars and began to pray for a healthy pregnancy and safe delivery.

In October of 2015, I found myself sitting in a neurologist's office with my mom and dad. I was hoping for good news, for comforting words that everything was going to be alright with my mom – but it was not to be. Even though I did not want to hear the truth, I had to come to terms with it. My mom was at the beginning of a long and painful decline that could take years as Alzheimer's would slowly take her away from me – and there was nothing I could do to stop it. While the loss of my brother was sudden and crushing, the loss of my mom would be a slow and steady chipping away, bit by bit, piece by agonizing piece. I was searching for hope, for a silver lining, but coming up short.

On January 25, 2016, exactly eight months after my brother's death, my precious niece was born. In the months leading up to her birth, a new friendship had been rekindled between my sister-in-law and me. We were closer than we had ever been before. We now had something in common that I never could have anticipated – motherhood. She sent me pictures of my niece from the other side of the world. How I longed to be there with them, to hold the baby, a piece of my brother in the flesh. How I longed to help her as she learned the ropes of being a first-time mom without him there to help her. She was a warrior and an inspiration. She did what many women would not have the strength or wherewithal to do, raising a child on her own while experiencing tremendous grief and pain.

In the months that followed, I watched online as my niece began to grow and change. She was beautiful and brought much joy to my heart. My own children brought me tremendous joy as well, a daily dose of joy, laughter, and purpose. God knew exactly what I would need to get me through those dark days and He provided what I needed through all my children. It wasn't long before I was emailing my sister-in-law to share some news with her. I was expecting our fifth child that December.

Back in 2012, just after the birth of my third child, I was reading *Uncle Tom's Cabin*. When I came across the name Evangeline in the book, I was enthralled with her character. Her character was good, pure, and sweet. I loved everything about her and cried bitter tears when she died in the story. I resolved that if I ever had another daughter, Evangeline would be her name. On a cold December night in 2016, I looked at the sweet face of my newborn daughter, Evangeline Ruth, and smiled. Her name means, "She bears good news," and there could not have been a better time for some good news in my life. Her middle name is Ruth, after my dear grandmother who had such a tremendous impact on my life. This birth did something to me, reawakening something in my heart that had been shriveled up and forgotten for many months – *hope*.

Day in and day out, I fight my way through the pain. I try to parent my five children, homeschool three of them, and keep a sane house. My days are very full, but the sorrow still plagues me. I try to live life as a normal person would, but the sadness is always there, just beneath the surface of my "I'm fine how are you" veneer. This is my Ground Zero, and it is here that I found my own cross in the midst of life's wreckage, just as I had observed in New York City. It is here that God met me, and gave me a story to write.

In the past several years I have lost so much. It feels at times like my world has been ripped out from under me and yet, as I look back over my journey, I've somehow come out on the other side a stronger person, able to face and overcome life's most difficult struggles now more than ever before. Is this because of some inner strength I possess? Absolutely not! The only reason I'm standing on two feet today is because of the Lord's goodness to me. He saw fit to dig deep down into the pit where I had fallen and rescue me. He was that beacon of hope in the wreckage of my Ground Zero. The beauty of His word and His promises to me shined in my heart on my darkest nights. I felt His peace enveloping me at the very times I was at the end of my rope.

He's given me a platform from which to speak, though it is surely not a platform I ever would have chosen. I am able to share my story because *I have suffered*. And in the midst of that suffering, God gave me a message comprised of some simple but profound truths that will help you if you are at your own Ground Zero.

My writing comes straight from the heart. God places things on my heart to write and on those days when I am not listening for what He has to say to me or not in His word, I can't write at all. I'm here for a purpose and one small thing I can do to make a difference in this world is to share some of my own struggles and triumphs with you. A passage that has been a tremendous help to me is found in Habakkuk 3:17-19 (AMPC):

Though the fig tree does not blossom and there is no

fruit on the vines, [though] the product of the olive fails and the fields yield no food, though the flock is cut off from the fold and there are no cattle in the stalls, Yet I will rejoice in the Lord; I will exult in the [victorious] God of my salvation! The Lord God is my Strength, my personal bravery, and my invincible army; He makes my feet like hinds' feet and will make me to walk [not to stand still in terror, but to walk] and make [spiritual] progress upon my high places [of trouble, suffering, or responsibility]!

In the pages to come, I will describe and share some anecdotes from my daily life. As God placed these thoughts on my heart, I realized they were the beginning of a story – a story of how God brought me through my darkest hours and into a deeper faith in Him. The beauty in this is that I have found hope, even in the middle of these difficulties. May these stories touch and bless your heart and encourage you through your own trials.

I would like to first dedicate this book to my mom, who is courageously in the fight of her life right now. She battles Alzheimer's and has lost both her sons, yet she still finds a reason to smile and enjoy life as best she is able. She taught me what it is to work hard, be strong, and have a real and lasting faith in God. She always encouraged me to excel at writing, and I am producing this book in response to her constant encouragement. Without her, I would not be the person I am today.

I would also like to dedicate this book to my brother Ed who, though he will never read it, would be proud of my efforts to write. He was tragically taken from this earth at the age of 31 on May 25, 2015 in that horrible rock-climbing accident. I've missed him every day since. He left behind a beautiful wife and an adorable little daughter who he never had the chance to meet.

Family prayer at dinner
(Photo courtesy of Kelly Krabill 2017)

SECTION ONE

A SEASON OF PAIN

Then I would still have this consolation—
my joy in unrelenting pain—
that I had not denied the words of the Holy One.

Job 6:10

Chapter 1
Hard Pressed but not Crushed

I never gave much thought to having a childlike faith and what that would look like until I had children of my own. I always knew I wanted to have children, but never imagined how profoundly they would impact my life. When I observe the ways my children respond to life, it often gives me great hope. Their outlook is so sunny; their trust in those who care for them is absolute. They forgive readily and hold no grudges. Their joy is as evident as the smiles that stretch across their faces when a beloved family member walks into the room.

Up until the day I gave birth to my first child, I thought parenting was all about teaching and taking care of someone else – but I had much to learn. Throughout my seasons of joy and grief, my greatest inspiration has been my children. Day in and day out, they teach me how to grow closer to God. At the end of the day, there is often a story, or incident that happened during the day that sticks in my mind and causes me to reflect on some aspect of my relationship with my heavenly Father.

For years, I've been writing down these stories, seeking to capture some of this inspiration on paper, hoping it can remind me as I someday look back over the years that throughout all my seasons, God was always at work. Even in my darkest moments, I occasionally get a glimpse of His plan and can see things fitting together in a way that suddenly makes sense. I haven't seen the whole picture yet, but I know this: It is a masterpiece.

When life seems to be pressing down on you harder than you can bear, come to Him in childlike faith. Resist the urge to fix your own problems and fight your own battles. Accept the gift of His love, just as children expect parents to love them. We can also learn from one of Jesus' lessons that involved young children:

> Jesus called a little child to him and put the child among them. Then he said, "I tell you the truth, unless you turn from your sins and become like little children, you will never get into the Kingdom of Heaven. So anyone who becomes as humble as this little child is the greatest in the Kingdom of Heaven" (Matthew 18:2-4 NLT).

1. Cancer

I was just six years old, standing alone in front of the entire congregation on a Sunday morning. My mom had spent weeks working with me at the piano in our living room, helping me to learn the words to the old hymn, "*Holy, Holy, Holy.*" There was no music accompanying me that morning, the room seemed so very quiet. I took a big breath and began to sing in my best, quivering six-year-old voice.

"Early in the morning, my song shall rise to Thee..."

I could not imagine then what those words would mean to me one day. My faith at that point was so simple and untested. I could not have envisioned a day when my mornings were spent on my knees in prayer, begging God for strength to carry on, praying for peace in the midst of great pain, and asking for healing needed by my loved ones.

"Holy, Holy, Holy! Merciful and mighty..."

Yes, God has poured out His mercies on me! And for what purpose and reason? What had I done, have I ever done, to deserve them? One aspect of God's mercy was the mother He blessed me with. She modeled what it was to be a godly woman and to have a relationship with Him. It became a common sight to see Mom up early, reading her Bible and praying – probably for me! The Lord was already preparing me for the battles of life shortly to come, girding me with His strength to endure the storm that was forming.

I was 12 years old, sitting in a hard, uninviting, waiting-room chair with my feet barely touching the linoleum floor. The clock ticked loudly, and the minutes passed as if in slow motion. I had just undergone a week of more tests than I knew existed. I had an MRI, a bone scan, full-body x-rays, and had blood drawn multiple times for a full gamut of tests. As we awaited the results from all this, the doctor finally came into the small examination room accompanied by a nurse. There was little prelude to his announcement; he merely stated,

"It's cancer."

The world seemed to come crashing down all at once, "Wait, what? *Cancer*? How is it even possible?" My mom sat beside me crying. I was too young and naïve to understand the implications or the way forward. I heard strange-sounding words like operation, biopsy, and chemotherapy, and none of it seemed real.

That night, my mom was on the phone for hours, sharing the news, asking for prayers from family and friends. I listened, but it seemed like she was talking about someone else and not me. Then cards started to arrive in our mailbox: cards of encouragement, cards with promises to pray, funny cards, and serious cards. One of my father's co-workers had his child's entire class of grade-schoolers send me handmade cards from Missouri. I still have a stack of those cards today, hanging on to the get-well wishes because they remind me of a time when my situation seemed desperate, but God carried me through.

After a week of going through more test results, my mom decided to take me to another hospital for a second opinion. I remember the second doctor well, and remember the overwhelming relief that flooded over me when he said it had all been a misdiagnosis. I had a rare condition in my knee that presented on the x-rays as a tumor, but it was in fact completely benign and required no action whatsoever. The pain I had been experiencing would gradually diminish as I continued to grow. I was fine!

Looking back, I marvel at this whole ordeal that lasted a week, but challenged me to the core of my young being. I wonder how seriously I would have taken my faith if this had not happened to me. I wonder how different my life would have been had I not been tested so early and caused to view life in a way not typical for a 12-year-old.

I was given the rare opportunity, at a very young age,
to see life in all its fragility, and to emerge wiser but unscathed.

The false alarm brought me to a crossroads with two choices or paths. I could continue with my life as I had been going, or I could view my newfound health as a gift and opportunity to do more with my life. I chose the second path. I began to dig into the Bible and seek God's will for my life. Of course, I was young and immature, but God was working, always pointing out to me the urgency and frailty of my human condition. He always nudged me to act now, rather than put things off to the future.

I chose to live with excellence, to set high goals for myself, and to push myself beyond what I thought I was capable of doing, for His glory. I had worry lines across my forehead at the age of 12, which spoke volumes of the burdens I had already carried. Instead of proceeding with my life as I had been going, however, I chose to rededicate myself to the Lord. I wanted to learn and live out His Word, and to serve Him in any way possible.

2. A Peace that Passes Understanding

I stood in front of a class of over 430 graduates at my high school graduation, one of three valedictorians who would give a speech. Four long years and countless hours of reading books and studying notes had earned me that distinction. It was not intelligence, but pure grit and determination that got me to that point.

I had never written a speech before and had no idea where to start. When it was my turn, I spoke not only of future hopes and dreams, but also about a recent school shooting. It was a somber subject to bring up, but even then I was using my platform to share how fleeting and uncertain life could be. I urged my classmates not to take any of life for granted, and commissioned them with a verse from 1 Timothy 4:12: "Don't let others look down on you because you are young, but set an example, in your speech, in life, in love, in faith and in purity."

That shooting had been an event that barely touched my life, but three years later I would have another encounter with death that was much closer to home. It was the morning of my twenty-first birthday, but this would be a day for a different kind of celebration. I was jarred from sleep as our telephone rang at 6 AM. When I picked up the phone, I heard the urgency in my grandmother's voice: "Come soon, there's not much time left. Grandpop is dying."

I went to wake my mother to give her the news about her dad. She quickly prepared to leave, but I hesitated. *Could I handle this? Was I ready to witness the passage from life into death?* The previous few weeks had been an emotional rollercoaster for me as I got permission from my Grove City College professors to take all my finals early so I could be at home with my family. Cancer had overtaken my grandfather's body and we knew that his time was short; the time had arrived.

I made up my mind to go, joining my aunts and uncles in my grandparents' bedroom that morning. My grandfather, the patriarch of our family, lay on a hospital bed, covered with blankets. He was a tall man in stature and strong in character, the moral bedrock of our family. His work ethic and desire to stay active kept him busy at odd jobs into his early eighties. In their bedroom, I watched his faltering breaths get weaker and further apart, until finally, he breathed his last.

It made me think of what Peter wrote in 1 Peter 1:24-25: "All people are like grass, and all their glory is like the flowers of the field; the grass withers and the flowers fall, but the word of the Lord endures forever." Peter used the simile that our lives are like grass, here and healthy today, but dried up and gone tomorrow.

I watched my grandfather's peaceful passing and thought of all his years, the memories I would have of him, and the legacy he created and left.

I remembered my grandfather's strong arms as he tossed my small frame into the water again and again in our backyard swimming pool. I remembered the way he used to hold my arms and take me out into the ocean when I was small, lifting me up over the waves just as they were crashing down. He exuded strength. That image of the crashing waves and being lifted over them always reminds me of the way that God carries me through my own trials. The thrashing and violent seas threaten to overtake and crush me, but He lifts me over those waves, shielding me from the brunt of their fury. I felt great pain at the loss of my grandfather. How do you ever feel ready to say goodbye to someone you love dearly?

In the midst of the pain, however, there was also an inexplicable peace. This was my first encounter with a peace that passes all understanding as described in Philippians 4:4. Faith can only be proven once it is tested. Athletes can only say they are ready for a race when they have trained for it. This death was one more test in my young life and there were many more to come. This ordeal was a chance for me to walk out and prove my faith.

Many welcome their twenty-first year with special celebrations, but for me, that milestone provided another sobering realization that life is fleeting. Yet in a more important sense, there was a celebration going on that day. As we were still processing his passing, my grandmother leaned forward to kiss him one last time, squeezing his hand and saying in her soft and sweet voice, "Goodnight, Sweetheart. I'll see you in the morning." There it was! A confident assurance, an inexplicable peace that comes from *faith*. There was no doubt in her voice as she spoke those words. It wasn't a sweetly uttered sentiment but a statement of fact. She *would* see him again one day. Visions of his ascent into heaven that morning, of the angels welcoming him at the pearly gates and celebrating his long-anticipated arrival, filled me with peace.

Fast forward 16 years. I have a baby balanced on my hip,

my three-year-old clamors for a drink, my five-year-old is following me around with a brush and hair tie, demanding I braid her hair, and my two oldest kids are in a heated argument. The smell of burned bread reaches my nose and I rush to the kitchen to try and save a grilled cheese sandwich from certain demise. Thirteen years of marriage and five children later, this is my new normal. My days are a blur. From 6 or 7 AM (if I'm lucky) until midnight, I am involved in cooking, cleaning, working through home school lessons, playing outside, doing laundry, and chauffeuring the kids here and there. I love it, well, not every second of it, but I do love it. I am blessed to be at this point in my life.

As I look back over the last four years, I realize my faith walk has taken some unexpected turns. There have been precipitous plunges and glorious mountaintops. God has taught and reiterated one basic need in my darkest hours, and that is to trust Him. He has repeatedly used my five children to teach me about life and faith. Their inquisitiveness, stubbornness, and joy have given me visions of my relationship with my own heavenly Father. When tempted to utter, "This is not fair," I have tried to step back and look at my life from His perspective, to see what He is trying to teach me. That is not always easy. Losing a friend and a brother, while at the same time seeing my mother endure great suffering, have brought me again and again to my knees in prayer. God has challenged me to have a childlike faith, to trust Him in all circumstances, and to relinquish my desire for control. The journey is far from over. There is much work to be done. I have never shied away from hard work, but I never imagined what hard work *faith* would be.

3. Holding on Tight

"She doesn't fear bad news. She confidently trusts the Lord to take care of her" (Psalm 112:7 NLT Paraphrase).

Do I confidently trust in the Lord to care for me? Do I allow Him full reign over my life, possessions, and family? Watching my son Lawson at the store gave me a glimpse of how I look to God.

I had foolishly ventured into the toy section of the store with all five children. Lawson squealed with delight as we passed by the aisle with the toy cars and trucks. His chubby little fingers clutched a fire truck toy with unwavering determination. He had found a prize and he was not about to leave it behind. His lip began to quiver and he immediately screamed as I pried it from his hands and placed it back on the shelf. It pained me to see him so unhappy and angry with me. As soon as I placed the truck back on the shelf, he grabbed another one right away, not willing to give up without a fight. As we left the store, I held him wiggling and unhappy. I placed him in his car seat and handed him some lunch, and he immediately grabbed the food and began gobbling it down. The thing he thought he needed so much was not actually the thing he needed most. I needed him to trust me to care for his needs. He needed to let go of the things he thought he needed and just trust me.

How often do I act just like my youngest son did that day, hanging onto things in my life that I think I can't live without? How often do I try to fight my own battles, unwilling to entrust the burdens I carry (or try to carry) to the One who is willing to be my Advocate and Defender? Two days in a row, I came across this verse in my daily reading time: "The Lord will fight for you, you need only to be still" (Exodus 14:14).

Be still...

How often could I honestly admit that I am still? Even when I am trying to be still, there are usually many other things running through my mind. I may think I'm trusting God to take care of me, but if I'm always thinking about "the next thing," always trying to plan everything out, unwilling to just let go. That represents a pretty conditional and limited sort of trust.

I've learned a lot of hard lessons about letting go. There were people I loved dearly who were taken away from me, and I never thought I could go on after those losses. I never imagined I'd be asked to let go of things of that magnitude. God is teaching me to trust in the midst of the pain from losing things I cherish. He is teaching me to relinquish my will and control and allow Him to direct my paths.

May we all hold on lightly to the things of this world, but grip firmly onto the truths of God. May we entrust everything to His care, and trust Him to fight our battles for us.

4. The Mind of God

Try as I may to climb out of this valley, I can't. The more I dwell on it, make plans and try to execute, the more I find myself slipping back down into the mire. I'm having a hard time climbing out from under this too-heavy yoke and letting Him handle it for me, but I know that is exactly what I must do.

You may find yourself in this situation as well, feeling like you are on a path you would never have chosen for yourself. Things aren't panning out the way you would have expected or wanted. You keep waiting for things to "get better." Maybe the issue isn't your circumstances but your perspective. Maybe this is exactly the way things are supposed to be. Maybe your perception of the "right" way your life should be going isn't right at all. Maybe you are clinging to the fire truck toy you think you need when you really need to trust that God your Father knows what you need, just like I knew what my son needed – and didn't need! Isaiah 55:8 runs through my mind: "'For my thoughts are not your thoughts, neither are your ways my ways,' declares the Lord."

How can I know the mind of God? How can I expect to understand His complex workings in my life? The difficult truth is, *I can't*, or often won't until well after the work is complete. It was only after my son received his lunch that he forgot about the truck. Therefore, I must keep surrendering up my will, desires, and demands to Him, and ask Him to give me His *peace*.

I must have faith that He knows what He is doing with my life and the lives of my loved ones. When I come to these moments of desperation, when I realize my human strength is really no stronger than a toothpick, I find myself falling on my face, crying out to the Lord for answers. And He answers, as He often does for me, through Scripture and in songs: "His grace is sufficient. His strength is made perfect in weakness" (2 Corinthians 12:9). I will keep hanging onto that truth for today.

5. Wounds that Cannot Heal

Throughout my life, I find myself in difficult situations. Sometimes it even seems that my trials will never end, that I will never find peace again, and never heal from hurts that afflict me. How do I press on in the midst of great suffering? How do I go so far, as Paul explained below, to exult or rejoice in my sufferings? I can't say that this is my natural human inclination:

> Moreover let us also be full of joy now! Let us exult and triumph in our troubles and rejoice in our sufferings, knowing that pressure and affliction and hardship produce patient and unswerving endurance. And endurance (fortitude) develops maturity of character (approved faith and tried integrity). And character [of this sort] produces [the habit of] joyful and confident hope of eternal salvation (Romans 5:3-4 AMPC).

When I'm faced with a situation that seems hopeless, where do I find the strength to go on? Is it perhaps necessary to go through these prolonged seasons of difficulty so that patient and unswerving endurance can be developed? The runner doesn't build endurance by going for a two-minute run every day. He certainly doesn't prepare for a tough race course by walking whenever he comes to a hill. No, he pushes himself to run farther and faster for months leading up to a race. He challenges himself physically, building up more and more strength over time.

I am realizing in these months and years of difficulty that when God doesn't remove a burden, I should not and cannot view it as a dead end. I can't react as if a door has been slammed in my face and retreat into pity and despair. He will use my wounds and difficulties to shape and prepare me for something much greater.

There may indeed be wounds in my life that will never heal. I may never have what I perceive to be a happy and carefree life, but is that really something to be desired? If being in a place of trial brings me closer to God, which I think it does, perhaps there can still be great joy, even in my deepest sorrow. My human inclination is not to turn to God on the days that run smoothly, but He comes to mind much more quickly on the days that are difficult.

I am learning to endure through the longest of days, knowing with full confidence there is a prize waiting for me at the end of this wearisome road. I look around and see so many others with me on this arduous journey. God has given us each other to encourage along the way. Therefore, press on, my dear friends, press on!

6. Insurmountable Odds

My son Lawson gave me a beautiful visual image of the way God enables us to overcome seemingly insurmountable odds. I appreciate how He can use everyday situations to speak to us in the midst of our trials. I love how He understands our human limitations, and meets us in a way we can easily relate to.

As soon as we pulled up to the park the other day, a little voice from the backseat of the car screamed with delight, "*Basketball!*" Sure enough, beside the kids' playground sat a dilapidated basketball court, six hoops evenly spaced around a rectangle of cracked asphalt. He grabbed the only balls we had brought, a soccer ball and a rubber play ball, and took off toward the court.

As I watched him, I had to shake my head in wonder. There he stood in the middle of the court, surrounded by 10-foot-high hoops that must have seemed to him to tower into the sky. Completely undaunted, he lowered the ball and heaved it with all his might toward the hoop. Wherever the ball fell, there he ran to try again, moving from one hoop to the next. He fell down again and again, but his effort did not waver or relent.

I stopped him for a moment, red-cheeked and out of breath, to remove his coat so he could continue in more comfort. For at least 15 more minutes, he continued to shoot baskets.

Maybe he made one shot, but the excitement never faded, and he never got upset; he just kept trying. As a two-year old, he had a resolve that was enviable.

When faced by a challenge that seems too great, an obstacle that appears beyond the scope of my faith, strength, and courage, I sometimes falter. It's easier to turn my back and run, to pretend it's not there, to say I gave it my best, when I really just gave up.

As I watched my son embracing these obstacles, taking on a challenge that was too great for him, I could sense the Lord speaking to me even through some rusty old basketball hoops:

> *I give you My word, My promise not to give you anything beyond what you can handle. There will be days, perhaps even years, when it feels like you won't make a single "shot" – but you must keep trying.*

God's promises stand:

- I will neither leave nor forsake you (Deuteronomy 31:6).
- I know the plans I have for you (Jeremiah 29:11).
- I love you with an everlasting love (Jeremiah 31:3).

He seemed to beckon me to step out in faith.

> *Show Me that you still trust Me even when it seems like nothing is going your way, like the obstacles are just too great to overcome.*

This is what it truly means to have faith. I remind myself that if God is for me, who can be against me? (see Romans 8:31). And I take that first step.

7. Endurance

Therefore, since we are surrounded by such a great cloud of witnesses, let us throw off everything that hinders and the sin that so easily entangles. And let us run with perseverance the race marked out for us, fixing our eyes on Jesus, the pioneer and perfecter of faith. For the joy set before him he endured the cross, scorning its shame, and sat down at the right hand of the throne of God. Consider him who endured such opposition from sinners, so that you will not grow weary and lose heart (Hebrews 12:1-3).

We long for perfection, stability, and consistency in this life, a routine that we can predict and plan around. I'm realizing more with each passing year that hoping for those things is like grasping for the wind. I will continually be disappointed if I am hoping for those things here on earth.

Christ endured so much for us, for me. He did it all while I was still a sinner, under the harshest possible circumstances, for the most unworthy and ungrateful of people. He endured the cross and great opposition, truly demonstrating for us the way to run the race and run it well: "I have fought the good fight, I have finished the race, I have kept the faith" (2 Timothy 4:7).

At the end of the day, when sadness threatens to strangle any joy I might have, when the heavy weight of this fallen world presses down on my heart, I turn to the One who has promised to give me rest, the One who restores my soul, and the One who brings joy, even in the midst of unbelievable sorrow. He wanted me to see that life is not meant to be easy. That is the reason He lived here with constant pressure and pain, and with only the barest of necessities provided for Him. He had to entrust everything to His Father during His years in ministry, and trust for even His basic needs of food and shelter. He endured it all and did so with grace.

I am tempted to throw up my hands and say, "Life just isn't fair! Why is this so hard? Why all this pain?" Then I turn to the One who endured, the One who was so much more justified in saying those things, but never did. He endured for me and you – let that fact soak into your heart and mind for the next few minutes. He endured that we might also endure, knowing we will experience the utmost joy when we reach the finish line and join Him in heaven one day. Press on, dear brothers and sisters! Throw off all that hinders and press on:

Forgetting what is behind and straining toward what is

ahead, I press on toward the goal to win the prize for which God has called me heavenward in Christ Jesus (Philippians 3:13-14).

8. Weary

Are you weary?
Do you feel worn down and discouraged?
Why does God sometimes allow you and I
to stay in a place of very deep pain?

I try to erect flood walls to hold back the sorrow in my heart, but it sweeps over me at times like a tsunami. When that happens, I find the words of Isaiah 50:4 especially helpful: "The Sovereign Lord has given me His words of wisdom, so that I know how to comfort the weary. Morning by morning He wakens me and opens my understanding to His will" (NLT).

I recently re-read the story of Paul and Silas when they were thrown into prison in Acts 16. They endured a brutal beating and were placed in stocks in a jail cell. One would think that they would be incapacitated, and in too much pain to do anything but the most basic of human functions, like eat or sleep. Luke, who wrote the book of Acts, recounted how at this point, where there would seem to be little cause or reason to rejoice, that this is just what they did: Paul and Silas were praying and singing praises to God, and others were taking notice! When an earthquake caused the prison to shake so much that the doors flew open and the chains of every prisoner fell off, they stayed put. They could have escaped, but instead stayed and shouted to the jailer who was on the verge of killing himself, "We are all here!"

I too have a responsibility to God to respond to my own circumstances in a way that glorifies Him. Why does He allow me to experience pain, weariness, trials, and tests? When my situation is at its darkest, my light will shine for others to see most brightly. I shout out, even in the midst of my pain, "I am still here! I'm not going anywhere. Use me, God, even now, to be a help, an encouragement, and a light to the world around me." I am weary, completely vulnerable, but I am not crushed! Morning by morning, He reminds me of this. It has become a day-by-day, sometimes minute-by-minute choice to trust Him.

When I read what Paul wrote, I get the idea he was at the same place as I am:

> But we have this treasure in jars of clay to show that this all-surpassing power is from God and not from us. We are hard pressed on every side, but not crushed; perplexed, but not in despair; persecuted, but not abandoned; struck down, but not destroyed (2 Corinthians 4:7-9).

Chapter 2
The Edge
of Greatness

I grew up just a 40-minute drive from the New Jersey shore. Summers were spent making many trips to our favorite beaches along the coast. The salt water, the sea air, and the vast ocean, stretching out as far as the eye could see, captured my heart. My parents were married on the beach, and they named me, their firstborn child, Shelley, like the many seashells they collected and brought home over the years.

I always found serenity at the beach, closeness with God that I could not experience anywhere else. Standing on the beach, with the surf lapping at my feet, I could gaze out into the seemingly endless ocean and marvel:

- Even the wind and the waves obey Him (Matthew 8:27).

- His precious thoughts outnumber the grains of sand on the seashore (Psalm 139:18).

I would ask myself: Who is this great God? How do I fit into His plan for the world around me? How do I come to terms with a God so mighty, so wondrous, and so much greater than my tiny mind can comprehend?

The words of Job ring true in my mind today: "Though he slay me, yet will I hope in him" (Job 13:15). My journey to understand more of God has only been accelerated by suffering being introduced into my life. Suffering has brought me to a place where I truly *need* Him, and He has not disappointed me. He brings order, reason, and purpose to me like the predictability of the rising and receding tides. His power, like the mighty crashing waves, humbles me. His glory, like the sun's first appearance on the ocean horizon, is stunning. I try but fail to comprehend the hundreds of miles of ocean that stretch out in front of me when I'm standing on the beach.

Late one night and far from any ocean shore, I paused to reflect on God's greatness once more. A deep sense of all I had lost threatened to engulf me and yet, in the midst of this, I had a deeper sense still of all that I have *gained*. It made no sense! How can this be, God?

He gently and lovingly reminded me that there is so much I will never understand. I can never fully appreciate or understand His greatness, but it is just the simple awareness of it that brings me into a closer relationship with Him. I have traveled around this country and witnessed some awesome sights. One time, I stood at the edge of the Grand Canyon, trying to comprehend the mile of space between me and the bottom. While standing there, I was terrified of getting too close to the edge. It clearly was not safe! The dizzying fear gripped my heart so intensely that it threatened to bring me to my knees.

That is a similar reaction to my limited ability to grasp God. He knew that my capacity to understand Him was exactly the size of a humble manger, and so He came in a form to fit that very size. He made Himself humble and approachable, all for me! There was no other way I could fully come to terms with who He was or have the kind of relationship I do with Him. Did He need to do this? He could have left me there, at the edge of the cliff, shrinking back in terror. Instead, He met me in a way more real and life-changing than I could have ever imagined.

Today, when I stand at the edge of His greatness I am able to do so without fear. He will not let me fall. I will stand and marvel at the magnificence of His love – and His creation!

9. Standing at the Edge of Greatness

"What is a Great Lake, Mama?" "Why is it so big?" "But this doesn't look like a lake, it looks like the ocean." "Are there any seashells in it?" "Why can't we see the other side?"

It was a long drive home after a weekend away. We decided to make a rest stop at a scenic little spot in Barcelona, New York. The kids got their first real glimpse of one of the Great Lakes, Lake Erie. It was neat to see their reactions, to see their glee as they dipped little toes into that majestic body of water. They had so many questions, and I could see the answers processing in their minds. As we stood there on a narrow and unassuming little beach, the vast lake stretching out before us, I thought about human perspective and how small our understanding really is. Our ability to process the vastness of God's glory, of His power, and of His love for us is so feeble, so meager, so inadequate.

I try again and again to understand things, to find meaning, reasons, and purpose in the things that trouble and perplex me. I attempt to make things fit into a formula that to me seems right. I see myself, a tiny speck of humanity, standing on a beach before a vast body of water stretching farther than my eyes can see. The water is God. I can see Him, but not all at once. His Greatness overwhelms me.

Meet me on that shore, oh God. Don't let me flounder in those shallow waters of doubt, fear, and discouragement. Don't let me stumble on the entanglements of worry, sorrow, and pain. There is much I do not understand. I must accept it in pure, childlike faith.

And yet, even in the midst of my human limitations, He floods my spirit with a wave of peace. He meets me there on the shore. His greatness doesn't disappoint when I cry out for help, for He sends a lifeboat in the form of His Son to rescue my sinking soul. I stand at the edge of His greatness. His grasp on me is secure, unwavering, and reliable. He lifts me up over the churning waves, reminds me of His ever-present help in times of trouble. This image of Him gripping me firmly takes me back to those wonderful days at the beach with my grandfather lifting me up and over the waves.

Give me but a glimpse beyond the veil of this tired and weary earth, God. Let my ears catch just a whisper of Your voice, and my eyes the faintest glimmer of Your glory.

10. Caretaker

Each summer, a day my kids keenly anticipate is the hatching of our first Monarch butterfly, an insect regal and full of splendor. The process begins with an egg hunt, which involves piling the excited kids into our van and driving along country roads near our home, looking for patches of milkweed. When we spot it, we pile out of the car to peek under the leaves in the hope of finding some of the microscopic eggs of a Monarch, or perhaps an already hatched Monarch caterpillar. We bring the eggs or caterpillars home to feed and care for them until they are ready to be released back into the wild, this time as an adult butterfly.

Lawson with a newly-hatched Monarch butterfly

The kids revel in this chance to see up close a true creature of beauty. I watch them, appreciating the experience from the perspective of the "caretaker." They enjoy watching the process from the hatching of the tiny egg all the way to the mature butterfly. Along the way, there is plenty of bug-jar cleaning, milkweed replenishing, and waiting – then waiting some more. The hard work is all worth it when that beautiful butterfly arrives. The miracle overshadows the process.

I have read this passage below many times but only meditated on the first half. Recently, it was the latter half that caught my attention:

> But he knows the way that I take; when he has tested me, I will come forth as gold. My feet have closely followed his steps; I have kept to his way without turning aside. *I have not departed from the commands of his lips; I have treasured the words of his mouth more than my daily bread* (Job 23:10-12, emphasis added).

Instincts tell a Monarch to lay her eggs on the milkweed plant, and the caterpillar to eat only those particular leaves and molt its skin multiple times. Instinct tells it when to shed its skin one final time and become a pupa, and in about 10 days it emerges an entirely new and beautiful creature. The complexity and delicacy of this process are amazing and can teach us so much.

The testing we encounter throughout our lives seems painful and at times meaningless and detrimental. We fail to see the bigger picture, which is the transformation that is occurring in us, the testing that results in pure gold. Were I to follow the advice in this verse from Job and truly treasure His words more than my daily bread, how much more would I be transformed?

When I try to envision my life from God's perspective as my Caretaker, I would see what it is like for Him as He nurtures and cares for me. He's always cleaning up after me, and my life seems awfully messy these days. He wants to make a complete transformation in my life, and day by day He's urging me forward toward that goal.

I can't stay the same; I've got a lot more growing to do. Though everything around me may fade away, though people will fail me and life will continue to surprise, confuse, and challenge me, I can continue to trust in Him and His unfailing Word, which is my sustenance and literal daily bread: "Jesus answered, 'It is written: 'Man shall not live on bread alone, but on every word that comes from the mouth of God'" (Matthew 4:4).

11. Survival

Huddled together on our backyard hill during a brief rain shower, my three kids sat giggling. When I walked over and peeked beneath the large golf umbrellas they sat under to ask what they were doing, they told me, "We're playing Survival."

"Oh okay," I said, "What do you do in Survival?"

"We have our tent to hide under."

I went back inside only to find my daughter Sienna grabbing lollipops out of the pantry. "Now what are you doing?" I inquired.

"We need lollipops," she told me emphatically.

A few minutes after that, I checked on them again. "What are you doing now?"

"We're eating leaves now and camouflaging ourselves!" Oh no they aren't, but yes they were. They were eating leaves off a tree in our backyard and coloring their faces, hands, legs, and feet with markers.

I *pause*. A somber moment hits me throughout the day every day now when I realize that someone very dear to me is no longer present on this earth. When that occurs, I begin my own game of Survival. I will need more than an umbrella, leaves, and a lollipop to make it through. I need strength, and not just human strength. I will need strength that can only come from the Lord.

Psalm 121:1-2 says, "I lift my eyes to the mountains - Where does my help come from? My help comes from the Lord the maker of Heaven and earth."

12. Seven Jars of Jelly

Hope is a perplexing and difficult thing. How can I find hope in the midst of great suffering? Again and again, the Bible teaches me that I can find it. Just a few years ago, I would never have understood the full impact of this truth. I would not have had the life experiences to fully grasp that concept of waiting for hope. Today, I understand it all too well.

When I experience a loss, when the thin facade of good health, financial security, the family unit, stability and predictability is shattered – that is when I fully realize what it means to hope, even in the face of adversity.

My husband and the kids harvested grapes from our backyard "vineyard" at the end of summer. Our lone grape plant had survived an early frost and several mauling attempts from our neighborhood bunnies. This one plant yielded more than six pounds of shiny purple grapes. There was just one problem: Their taste was not nearly as good as their outward appearance. When we bit into every single little grape, we discovered a center with at least three or four seeds. The skin was rather tough and the taste was a mix of sour and sweet. All those months of waiting with high expectations led only to disappointment.

Or maybe not? Perhaps there was another purpose for them: grape jelly. The grapes had to be washed and sorted. My husband discarded the bad ones, then pulverized and boiled the good ones, after which we strained out all of the skins and seeds. It was quite a process and required hours of work for only seven small jars of grape jelly. The final form of those grapes bore no resemblance to the original tantalizing bunches growing on the vine. They had to go through a long and arduous process to reach their final form.

I liken my own life experiences to that process as I sit and mull over it. Who I was a few years ago is not the person I am today. I've had to undergo a total redefinition, and I am still undergoing that redefinition, dare I say transformation. My life has taken on a form unlike anything I ever expected or planned it to have. The things I expected to happen and the things I hoped for previously have changed dramatically.

There have been many dark days when I experienced hopelessness as the things outside my control commanded my thoughts and emotions. I longed for answers that didn't come, and an end to the pain I felt daily. Trusting in the Lord, even when it seems there isn't any hope, is the hardest lesson I've had to learn.

In a few moments of quiet reflection, Romans 8:37-39 came to mind. Nothing, absolutely *nothing* can separate me from God's love. I still have a promised and wonderful hope. I reflect on the greatness of God and realize that His plan, though confusing at times, is perfect. The refinement and transformation process is far from over. There may still be years of waiting with questions unanswered and pain to endure. My weaknesses, insufficiency, and inability to find hope on my own all remind me to keep going back to God, the Sustainer of my hope and Refiner of my soul. Nothing on earth can separate me from the love of God:

> No, in all these things we are more than conquerors through Him who loved us. For I am convinced that neither death nor life, neither angels nor demons, neither the present nor the future, nor any powers. Neither height nor depth, nor anything else in all Creation, will be able to separate us from the love of God that is in Christ Jesus our Lord (Romans 8:37-39).

13. Keeper

My kids love to try on their older siblings' shoes, clothes, and sports gear. As soon as the keeper gloves came out, my younger son Lawson and daughter Sienna were vying for them, eager to take their turns playing goalie. As you can imagine, the (at that time) one-year-old and three-year-old with gloves about four sizes too big weren't the most effective goalkeepers, but they were trying their hardest!

Watching the little ones try to defend their goal from oncoming kicks gave everyone a good chuckle. They had all the

Lawson with his keeper gloves – ready to defend

passion and intensity of an Olympic goalie, but their efforts sadly fell far short. It reminded me of a passage I'm memorizing with the kids about putting on the full armor of God.

> Put on the full armor of God, so that you can take your stand against the devil's schemes. For our struggle is not against flesh and blood, but against the rulers, against the authorities, against the powers of this dark world and against the spiritual forces of evil in the heavenly realms. Therefore put on the full armor of God, so that when the day of evil comes, you may be able to stand your ground, and after you have done everything, to stand.

> Stand firm then, with the belt of truth buckled around your waist, with the breastplate of righteousness in place, and with your feet fitted with the readiness that comes from the gospel of peace. In addition to all this, take up the shield of faith, with which

you can extinguish all the flaming arrows of the evil one. Take the helmet of salvation and the sword of the Spirit, which is the word of God. And pray in the Spirit on all occasions with all kinds of prayers and requests. With this in mind, be alert and always keep on praying for all the Lord's people (Ephesians 6:11-18).

In a world that is turbo-charged with controversy and strife, violence and racial inequalities, wars and terrorist attacks, how can we possibly find peace? We need to remember first and foremost that our battle is "not against flesh and blood." It is easy to attack a neighbor, a friend, a family member, a public figure, or a politician. When we do, we are targeting the wrong enemy.

How do we prepare for life's toughest onslaughts? We innately desire peace, calm, good health, predictability, comfort, and routine. We soon realize, however, that we cannot expect these things in this life. More often than not, they are the exception rather than the norm.

I can see the devil cackling with glee as his attacks are met by people who are wearing keeper gloves four sizes too large rather than putting on the armor of God. We often aren't aware of his approach. He catches us off-guard when we are tired, distracted, when we are pointing fingers of blame at other people, or when we find ourselves in a dark time. He knows just how and when to strike, render us defenseless, and quickly defeat us.

Not only do we need to recognize our enemy and wear the right gear, we also need to pray! "Pray on all occasions . . . with all kinds of prayers and requests . . . *and keep on praying.*" How often do I pray when confronted with a problem before trying to fix it myself? Not often enough!

There are days I start off on the wrong foot when I'm not properly geared up to face the onslaught of life. I'm ill-equipped and focusing on all the wrong things. God wants us to remember that if we find your strength in Him, He will not disappoint us, even on our worst days. We cannot win this fight on our own.

14. Contrasts

I am in a place of overwhelming darkness in which I cannot see my spiritual hand in front of me. I never imagined the pain of tragic and sudden losses and how dramatically they would affect and change my life forever. On the morning after my brother's passing, I felt completely surrounded by that darkness as if a cloud had enveloped me. I had to get out of the house for a run, as crazy as that may sound. As I pushed my body into motion, tears were streaming down my face, and suddenly I was unable to breathe. Is this what it feels like to be at the point of total hopelessness and despair? "Rescue me, God! Help me to draw another breath, help me to take another step, help me out of this pit!"

"Unto the upright there ariseth light in the darkness: He is gracious and full of compassion and righteous" (Psalm 112:4 KJV). How am I to find joy in the midst of sorrow, purpose in pain, and strength when all I feel is weakness? The power of God is most evident when I am confronted with these contrasts. I need the strength but all I can feel and see is the weakness. I can see Him working more clearly than ever when I acknowledge my need for Him during those difficult times. He shines as a light in the darkness. What more powerful image of contrast could be used to describe this phenomenon?

There are times when we have had a power outage at night. One of the kids is terrified of the darkness and will scream out in fear whenever this happens. He is instantly comforted when we bring even a dim light into the room. God brings that same kind of peace and comfort to us, even in the midst of our darkest moments. Just seeing even a small flicker of light brings hope, comfort, and a calm we can never find on our own.

When I awaken, usually quite early in the morning, I look out the window. Seeing the first light of day after the long, dark night is for me one of the most awe-inspiring experiences. That early light is so predictable that we often ignore and take it for granted. It reminds me, however, of the greatness of God: "Indeed, the heavens declare the glory of God" (Psalm 19:1). I pause to soak in the scene, and then reflect on Him and the plans He has for me. His compassion for me is far too vast for my own understanding. He pours new life into me when I cry out for help: "In Him we live and move and have our being" (Acts 17:28).

Chapter 3
Glimpses Beyond the Veil

I recognize more every day that my perspective is limited. The path I walk is not the one I would have chosen, but God can use our trials to shape us into better people in the end. Occasionally, He gives me "glimpses beyond the veil." It is difficult to explain this phenomenon, but I can be going about my day and in the midst of a routine task, I suddenly sense something much deeper, something supernatural. What surrounds me seems to fade away, if only for a moment, and I'm intensely aware in that moment of another reality that exists in parallel to my own.

There is a greater world than the bounds of this Earth on which I live. God is preparing my eternal home even now. What occupies my time here, though important, pales against what is to come. And the sufferings I endure here, though intensely difficult to bear at times, will pale one day when I finally see Him face to face. In the blink of an eye, all of this will be gone. In the blink of an eye, my life will be over, and only then will it truly begin.

This is difficult for me to understand and embrace because:

- I'd rather my brother had not died.
- I'd rather my mom was well again.
- I'd rather not be estranged from my other sibling.
- I'd rather my friend was not in jail for taking the lives of two of her children.

These things do not seem fair or logical. In an otherworldly sense though, I know deep down that I am a better person because of my sufferings. I would not be writing a book right now if my life hadn't played out the way it has. I wouldn't parent my children the way I do, appreciate the small things the way I do, be able to forgive the way I have, have patience, courage, or motivation. I can't imagine where I would be right now were it not for the horrible things that have occurred. Therefore, I can look at all that has happened and be thankful, not for the things themselves, but for the way God met me in the midst of my pain and carried me through it: "Give thanks in all circumstances; for this is God's will for you in Christ Jesus" (1 Thessalonians 5:18).

I am not some lowly pawn, going through the motions of life for a distant, withdrawn God who could care less about me. The sense I gain is always of His *love* for me; His concern, care, and compassion for me overwhelm me. My life means something to Him. While many ignore Him, turn their backs on Him, blame and accuse Him, they fail to recognize how deeply He loves them. If only we could see beyond the here-and-now and see how everything plays out, then many more things would make sense. To those of us who believe, He promises that someday it will all be made clear. Our eyes will finally be opened and our tears will flow no more. There will only be joy and that joy will be complete at last. For now, in spite of my doubts and lack of understanding, I choose to trust in the One who shepherds my soul.

15. In the Shadow of the Almighty

I encountered a terrifying scene one day when I was least expecting it. The kids were happily playing outside on a gorgeous, sunny day in late October. My oldest son and some friends were having a Nerf battle in the yard and Lawson who was two at the time was tagging along, running after them as best as he could. I tried to keep up with him but was having trouble chasing him around the house. For a minute, I lost sight of him and he was gone. He had stopped following the older boys and was nowhere in the backyard.

For some reason, I felt the need to go straight around to the front of the garage, and there he was. He had already dragged the jogging stroller out of the garage, I'm still not sure how, and was perched in the seat, at the top of our steep driveway. He was only seconds away from careening down our driveway, out into the street, and who knows to what end. I raced to him and grabbed him, my heart pounding not from exertion but rather fear. All day I replayed this scene in my head again and again. What if I hadn't found him when I did? Then I took consolation in two verses from the book of Psalms:

- Those who live in the shelter of Most High will find rest in the shadow of the Almighty. This declare about the Lord: He alone is my refuge, my place of safety; He my God, and I trust Him (Psalm 91:1-2 NLT).

- No evil will overtake you, no plague come near your home; He will order His angels to protect you wherever you go (Psalm 91:10-11 NLT).

I reflected on what it means to dwell in the "secret place of the Most High," or to "rest in the shadow of the Almighty".

It's easy to complain about things that aren't going our way or to focus on the bad things that happen throughout the day. We can easily take for granted all the things that are going right. We can write God off so quickly when things go wrong, thinking that He doesn't care about us, that He's ignoring our prayers and demands, or that our problems are too big for Him. What about all the times He is providing for us, for not only our most basic needs but performing everyday miracles, keeping us safe, healthy, and shielding us from harm?

I happened to read the comforting verses of Psalm 91 as I reflected on what could have happened to my son. They are verses that beckon the downtrodden or dissatisfied soul to trust in the Lord. How many times has He cared for me, times of which I wasn't even aware? How often has He saved me, my children, other friends or family from harm? How often have I thanked

Him for being a refuge for me? Acknowledged that He is sovereign over my life and the lives of the ones I love most?

I have peace when I remember and dwell on these truths that I can rest in His shadow, relying on Him to care for me.

16. Battles

"Though the fig tree does not blossom and there
is no fruit on the vines, [though] the product
of the olive fails and the fields yield no food,
though the flock is cut off from the fold and
there are no cattle in the stalls, Yet I will rejoice
in the Lord; I will exult in the [victorious] God
of my salvation! The Lord God is my Strength,
my personal bravery, and my invincible army; He
makes my feet like hinds' feet and will make me
to walk [*not to stand still in terror, but to walk*] and
make [spiritual] progress upon my high places [of
trouble, suffering, or responsibility]!"
(Habakkuk 3:17-19 AMPC).

When I discovered him in the shed, he was beside himself. He was tugging and pulling and near tears, trying with all his might to free the little bike he so badly wanted to ride on. No matter how hard he pulled, however, he simply couldn't free it; it was too heavy for him to move. I looked at my son Lawson with compassion and quickly came to the rescue, freeing the bike and carrying it out so he could ride it.

My children give me so many daily opportunities to visualize my own struggles in this life and the way my Heavenly Father watches over and intervenes on my behalf. Through them, I get tiny glimpses beyond the veil, a rare opportunity to understand in a small way what God might be trying to accomplish, even in the midst of great pain.

I may have all the best intentions and think I have the physical strength to overcome great difficulties, but at times I face a trial that is simply too great for me to handle on my own. The weight of the world presses down on me heavily and I feel its crushing presence, but I am powerless to respond. In a moment of prayer when I cry out to God for help, I feel the weight lift. I imagine Him, taking hold of this burden sitting on my shoulders like an enormous, heavy coat lifting it off me. He strengthens my feet, enabling me to walk again, even in the midst of the pain.

I never really stopped to think about what high places were and what it means to "tread on" them. The high places are the difficulties we face, and many times when I encounter difficulties, I falter. I lose my footing and confidence, and maybe I question God. The idea of walking with my head held high through these mountainous trials, of actually making spiritual progress in spite of them, is certainly something to dwell on and aspire to. If I'm relying solely on my own strength to accomplish this, however, I will fail. No, I need to rely on the strength that comes from the Lord. Then and only then will I be able to walk, without terror, on the high places.

No struggle is too great and no problem beyond His control. When He is fighting our battles for us, we can have peace, confidence, and *hope*.

17. Heartbreak and Broken-Hearted

Imagine yourself, anxious and afraid, sitting with your feet dangling over the edge of an examination table. You look with expectation toward the physician who is typing some notes on his laptop, brow furrowed in concentration, as you await his diagnosis. He then turns to you, and without hesitation says, "You have a heart condition."

Your body sags a little under the weight of this news, but it doesn't come as a complete shock to you. You've known it for quite some time for you were born with it. "What can I do?" you ask him. He looks at you, and with compassion and kindness in his eyes he says, "Realization and acceptance are the first steps to healing."

The heart condition I'm referring to here isn't something

unique to you. It's a condition that afflicts every one of us, a life-long, ever-present disease that eats away at our joy, peace, and ability to live and exist in this world, enjoying it in the ways we were intended to.

In my own life, I've discovered that it takes a heart break to recognize that I have a broken heart. It requires a situation that thrusts me far beyond my capacity to hope in order to help me realize the true condition of my flawed, human heart. I can only hide behind the guise of self-sufficiency for so long. Eventually I will encounter a situation that is too intense for me to withstand on my own strength. In those moments of despair, the true test begins, for that is when my innermost beliefs and tendencies are revealed for all to see as Jesus predicted: "For where your treasure is, there will your heart be also" (Matthew 6:21).

Had I not repeatedly sought the Lord, my heart would have given up or given out by now. I would have succumbed to the oft-tempting "solutions" of self-pity, or self-medication through food or material possessions. I would have fallen prey to total despair or great bitterness, but He gives me grace – *so much grace.*

He also brings pure and effervescent joy to my world that is often dim, dark, and desperate. He takes away my heart of stone and gives me a heart of flesh again as He promised: "I will give you a new heart and put a new spirit in you; I will remove from you your heart of stone and give you a heart of flesh" (Ezekiel 36:26).

Only by the grace of God have I been able to overcome the faltering, diseased condition of my heart. I cringe when I think of what my life might look like today had I not chosen to allow the great Physician to heal my heart. It is with total assurance that I can say His grace is sufficient; when I am weak, then I am strong as described in 2 Corinthians 12:10.

My heart has been broken again and again. It continues to be broken with each passing day because of this is fallen and imperfect world we live in. Thankfully, *I know* that my hope is not trusting in the things of this world. I pray that God would help you see your heart as it really is. Ask Him to allow you to experience glimpses of His love, His provision, and His plan for you.

18. Press On

"So let us know, let us press on to know the
Lord. His going forth is as certain as the dawn;
And He will come to us like the rain, like the
spring rain watering the earth" (Hosea 6:3).

This verse really grabs hold of my heart. There is little in this life that is truly certain. Much of what we cling to for our security is nothing more than shifting sand. Knowing God gives me so much peace and strength to overcome the difficulties in life. I appreciate the prophet's emphasis of *pressing on* to know Him. It takes hard work sometimes to pursue Him in a meaningful way. There are many distractions that pull me away from my time with Him.

He waters my parched soul with His grace, peace, and love for me. He brings me renewed hope and gives me reason to wake up each morning with His praises on my lips.

19. User Error

I try to frequently inventory the clothes hanging in my closet to see if there are any items that I no longer wear. One day, my gaze paused on a blue-striped shirt that I hadn't worn for quite some time, so I figured I'd give it one last chance. I tugged it on over my head in the pre-dawn, dimly-lit bathroom as I readied myself for another long day. Throughout the day, I would occasionally pull at the shirt because it didn't seem to fit any longer. By dinner time, my neck was feeling like it was in a noose and I concluded that this shirt was destined for the thrift store bin! Only then did I look down and see that I had the shirt on backwards. It took me the entire day to realize what was wrong!

You may be thinking I'm not the most observant person. The truth is that I was quick to lay the blame on something else; it could not be a problem with me. I was ready to get rid of a shirt when really it was just my own mistake.

How often in my life am I quick to misdiagnose a situation? How often do I look at a problem I'm facing and blame God for it, or question His reason for allowing it, only to discover down the road that it led to something far better in the end?

The words of Isaiah came to mind that night as I was falling into bed: "For My thoughts are not your thoughts, neither are your ways My ways, declares the Lord" (Isaiah 55:8). How quick we can be to dismiss God, His promises, and His word as true, relevant, and vital to our existence because things aren't lining up the way we think they should.

"This just doesn't fit my lifestyle. It isn't comfortable any longer. It isn't working out the way I think it should. Something just doesn't feel right to me." Those are all statements we make when we misdiagnose the true problem - we have our shirt on backwards.

Don't be so quick to dismiss Him. Don't be so self-assured that you miss out on a big blessing in your life. That same day, as I was out for thirty minutes of alone time jogging around the neighborhood, I ran into a neighbor friend who I hadn't talked to in a while. I slowed to walk with her for 10 minutes and as we rounded a bend, we both looked up at the sky. There were billowing black clouds all around, but throughout the clouds were openings with brilliant beams of golden sunlight shooting through. "That's like our lives," she told me – she who lost a husband and I who lost a brother. "If we can just get outside, it broadens our perspective on things," she concluded and I agreed.

Get outside of yourself – your preconceived notions about life and God, your tendencies to blame Him rather than accept His plan for your life. Walk with Him, regardless of what path it may take you on.

Submit to His perfect will. Accept that there will be some user error along the way. We imperfect humans tend to mess things up badly at times. Remember that our ways are not His ways. Learn from those moments when you are ready to give up and throw in the towel. Then turn to the One who has written the complete "Guide to Life and How to Live It." Grab hold of that users' manual and dig in to His amazing Word. Revel in the knowledge that He cares about you and has a plan for all of us: "I have a plan for you, says the Lord" (Jeremiah 29:11).

20. My Cup Runneth Over

I'm in a house with five kids, which means I'm used to spills. Not a day passes when there isn't some mini-disaster of a spill. One recent morning started with my son carrying a grass-filled sand bucket into the kitchen and dumping it all over the floor. He dutifully fetched the little hand vacuum, sucked up all the dirt, then immediately hit the canister release button, dumping out an even larger pile of dust, dirt, and sand all over the floor.

I realized that I've witnessed many epic, life-altering spills. I think about the comforting words in Psalm 23 and revel in the contrasts that walk hand in hand. One moment I'm "walking through the valley of the shadow of death," and the next, "my cup runs over." How can this be?

While many curse God in their trials, I'm reminded that sometimes He uses, not causes, those very trials to draw us nearer to him. I may walk through a deep, dark valley, but I know He is near; therefore, fear will not paralyze me. The phrase "my cup runs over" is an amazing visual of the way God blesses us. I'm un-deserving of even a few precious drops of His mercy, forgiveness, and love, yet He willingly and abundantly bestows them on me in overflowing quantities.

I was recently reading a passage from Daniel, paying close attention to what made him an exceptional follower of the Lord. What impressed me about Daniel is that he prayed *a lot*. He prayed three times a day, no matter what, even when he knew he could die for it. If only my prayer life looked something like that. How much more would I be able to appreciate the overflowing goodness of God if I connected with Him that regularly and with Daniel's devotion?

When you are having a bad day, it is tempting to view the glass as half empty. Maybe you need to pause and look a little more closely. Sometimes your greatest blessings are staring you right in the face. May my childrens' daily spills only serve to remind me of the overflowing goodness of God and of all the ways He continually blesses me, even in the midst of challenges and trials.

Chapter 4
Weeping May Endure for a Night

I've had my share of tear-filled nights. I cry out to God for help and though the sorrows do not diminish, I can sense that He is there. The psalmist wrote, "You keep track of all my sorrows. You have collected all my tears in your bottle. You have recorded each one in your book" (Psalm 56:8 NLT).

God cares! I never knew the depth of His caring until I was in my darkest hour. When I experienced grief that shook me to the core, it was then that His lovingkindness became ever more real to me.

If God truly cared, why would He allow all this in the first place? Why does human suffering occur under the watchful eye of a supposedly loving God? There is much that I still do not understand. I do know that even in the most perfect environment, the Garden, man chose to disobey God and introduced sin into the world. God gave us the free will to make choices on our own, and loves us enough to allow us to make choices that sometimes will cause us great pain. The brokenness of this world is the result of all that, but it is not the way He ever intended it to be.

I am hopeful because I know that in the end, God wins. He will put an end once and for all to this mess we've created.

He will welcome with loving arms those who have accepted and believed in Him, and then we'll finally experience things the way they were meant to be.

Even now, in the midst of my pain, I see cause for hope. He gives me the strength for each new day and shows me, again and again, pictures of life springing up from what was once dead, light shining in the darkness, and healing that comes out of brokenness.

21. Winter is followed by Spring

I've been watching them for weeks, just waiting for the day the tiny green leaves would give way to beautiful flowers, the first colors of spring erupting from the recently frozen, lifeless earth. There is something very special about the first flowers of spring. For months, everything is dead and shriveled up; then suddenly there is life again.

I revel in this cycle of seasons, and it gives me reason to pause and reflect over the long season of winter giving way to new life, fresh beauty, and delicate promises of the bounty of summer still to come.

I realized last spring that these flowers held a new and poignant meaning for me. The tulips blooming in my yard were a gift to me from my brother in 2012. He brought the bulbs back from a trip to Holland and gave them to me for Christmas that year. I've always enjoyed them and the thoughtfulness that accompanied them, but never imagined it would be mixed with the deepest sorrow. In 2015, I lost my brother, yet this gift lives on to remind me of him every spring.

Winter does always end. The warmth in the air and the breeze blowing with the scent of life is a testament to that. I look at the sweet faces of my children also radiant with new life and great promise. They beckon to me – carry on.

I must carry on even through the cold of winter. Life isn't meant to be an endless summer. There will be cycles of seasons throughout that serve to grow, teach, and make us appreciate the smallest of flowers even more. I'm thankful for the beauty of

My tulips from heaven

spring and for all signs of new life around me. Once again, I think of what the psalmist wrote: "Weeping may endure for a night, but joy comes in the morning" (Psalm 30:5).

22. The Super Bloom

The radio was on as I drove the kids to an appointment, and I heard an interesting news story. There was a rare phenomenon taking place in the California deserts called a super bloom. The flooding rains that soaked the state over the previous months caused this event to unfold, causing the driest places to burst forth with amazing colors. Even Death Valley was awash in color. Later that same night, I did some searching online for photos of the super bloom and was amazed to see the beautiful flowers covering the desert surface. One of the most desolate and inhospitable places on earth was alive with color.

I could not help but see the biblical parallels to this event. For more than a decade, delicate seeds have been sitting in hibernation, just waiting for the right conditions to bloom. Up to that point, the soil seemed barren, cracked, and for all intents and purposes, dead to any form of life. Those seeds, however, were there all that time, just waiting for their time.

In one video I watched, the park ranger describes it as a valley of death being transformed into a valley of life. This is an image of hope – that even the most barren wastelands can be transformed into a scene of phenomenal beauty. "*Yea, though I walk through the valley of the shadow of death.*" (Psalm 23:4)

There have been many days where my heart can scarcely bear the sorrow. This valley is deep and no end seems in sight. Today, I have a vision of the super bloom. I have no doubt in the midst of this great personal desert, seeds are being planted.

I wait in great hope and expectation for the day I will see God's hand working mightily, as described in Isaiah 35:6: "waters shall break forth in the wilderness and streams in the desert." I'm waiting for a super bloom when my own desert will be awash in color, when God's hand that is clearly working even in the midst of this dry season will be revealed in all its glory.

23. Love Never Fails

Love bears up under anything and everything
that comes, is ever ready to believe the best
of every person, its hopes are fadeless under
all circumstances, and it endures everything
[without weakening]. Love never fails [never
fades out or becomes obsolete or comes to an
end] (1 Corinthians 13:7-8 AMPC).

I watched as my mother held my sweet baby girl for the first time, a moment for me of intense joy intermingled with an aching heartbreak. My mother gave everything for me. She greeted me in the morning on days I needed to wake up early by coming into my room and gently pulling back my curtains while singing, "You are my sunshine." I wish I could somehow pay her back now for all that she did for me. I wish there was something I could do to help her during this most difficult time.

Losing my brother, her son, produced enough suffering for a lifetime. Now I am losing her too, and right now I ache to know why, to have some glimpse of God's plan. I ache for a miracle of healing for my mom and want to understand the timing of losing my mom right on the heels of losing my brother. While losing him was sudden and shocking, losing her has been agonizingly slow and tortuous. Day in and day out, I long for things to "get better" but they only get worse.

Love bears up under anything. *But God, why does there have to be so much hurt and sorrow? Why this pain that never seems to go away?*

Its hopes are endless under all circumstances. *God, there is still so much I have to learn, so much I truly do not understand, and so much of the bigger picture, of your plan, that I have yet to see.*

It endures everything without weakening. *Help me remember that when I am weak, then I am strong. Help me see You even on the most difficult days and not to take for granted all the blessings You have given me and still pour out on me, day after day.*

Love never fails! I will not be disappointed, discouraged, or dragged-down. The love of my heavenly Father was first demonstrated to me by my own parents who loved me. Becoming a parent has only heightened my awareness of what it means to love and be loved. And going through many trials and experiencing devastating loss have shown me that my hope, my one true hope, is in God, and *God is love.*

> "Yes, I have loved you with an everlasting love; therefore with loving-kindness have I drawn you and continued My faithfulness to you" (Jeremiah 31:3).

24. Hills and Valleys

> I lift up my eyes to the mountains—where does
> my help come from? My help comes from the
> Lord, the Maker of heaven and earth (Psalm 121:1-2).

Where do you set your eyes? When every possible distraction vies for your attention, how do you redirect your focus?

I had an opportunity to do a little gardening one afternoon. As I surveyed my flower beds, I realized that my bushes and trees were crowded, and that some things needed to be cut back or moved. The first "victim" was the Japanese maple tree, whose low-hanging branches got a much-needed pruning. Next, I turned my attention to a rose bush sandwiched between two larger holly shrubs. I marveled at the size of it, for only two years back I had dug up that same rose bush from its first home on our hillside. It was struggling to survive there and had only one rose bloom the entire year. The year after I moved it, it nearly doubled in size and produced many beautiful and fragrant roses. There I was again, shovel in hand, ready to dig it up, and this time not for being scraggly and under-productive but for growing too fast.

I jumped down on the shovel with both feet to loosen the roots, knowing I was certainly not going to be able to salvage all of them. I felt sorry for this poor bush that was going to undergo yet another traumatic transplant. I dug a new hole for it down by our mailbox. Next, I used the clippers to prune it back, trimming off many of the growing buds that would soon have been roses. It seemed unfair and an inopportune time to do that, but without this pruning, it would have had an even more difficult time rebounding from the move.

As I spent a few hours with my hands in the dirt, I began to ponder the similarities of growth and change, of beautiful blooms and difficult pruning seasons. There were similarities in my life and there probably are in your life too. I have experienced amazing highs and desperate lows. I've grasped at the wind for answers, trying to understand and cope, to somehow appreciate these seasons of life. Sometimes I succeed, sometimes I flounder, but my rate of success is fully dependent on where I set my eyes.

I know what I'm "supposed" to do, just like that rose bush that will instinctively keep on growing, despite the trauma I've put it through. I will keep growing as long as I am able to grow. Isn't that exactly what God wants for my life: to grow and push with all my might, even if I am only able to produce one meager rose in a growing season?

I serve a God of hills and valleys, but even in the deepest valleys, I keep my eyes on Him. I remember that suffering produces perseverance and that His joy will come in the morning.

SECTION TWO
THE NEED FOR RAIN

"Let my teaching fall like rain
and my words descend like dew,
like showers on new grass,
like abundant rain on tender plants."

Deuteronomy 32:2

Chapter 5
The Idea of Faith

I press myself as tightly up against the side of the bus as possible and look out the window, fear gripping my heart. A place that was once safe and comfortable for me is now awkward and terrifying.

Up until then, my routine consisted of climbing up the steps of the bus and hopping right into the front seat, safely by the bus driver. The bigger kids always sat in the back of the bus; that was not a place I would ever dare to venture. I was in second grade and was one of the smallest kids in my entire class. My teacher nicknamed me "Miss Mouse" that year.

But then everything changed. As a means of punishing one of the oldest and most meddlesome kids who was constantly getting into trouble, the bus driver came up with an excellent solution. He brought the boy to the front of the bus and had him sit next to me in the front seat from then on. I was petrified, and angry! What had I done wrong to deserve this sort of punishment? I got on the bus every day, went straight to that first seat, and sat quietly looking out the window until we arrived at school. Now my solitude was being interrupted by the tallest, meanest boy on the bus. I never wanted to step foot on that bus again.

Days and then weeks passed by, and my solitude of the front seat became a distant memory, but something else unexpected happened too. Once I was willing to edge away from the window just a bit and talk to that mean person next to me, a relationship began to form. One day as I climbed into my seat, there was no longer any fear. When pushed outside my comfort zone, I realized what I was truly capable of, and that eventually led to me becoming friends with the biggest bully on the bus.

No, he probably wouldn't have taken any notice of me if we'd crossed paths in the halls at school, but on that ride to school, we talked comfortably and joked around with each other like old friends. I also discovered that sometimes the way we initially perceive a person isn't always the whole picture, and that everyone deserves a second chance.

Let's fast forward to the present day. I sit in the front seat of my minivan, driving along a winding country road. A mild fall breeze blows in through the open windows. Multicolored leaves waft lazily through the air, making a slow-motion journey to their final resting place. Everything seems perfectly normal. The kids are amazingly quiet in their seats, enjoying the new books we've just picked up from the library. In the passenger seat next to me sits my dear mother.

The thought suddenly hits me that perhaps this will be our last trip to the library together. In spite of my prayers, I am losing my mother, day by day. The agony of this slow loss is almost unbearable. *"Why, God, oh why is this happening? What have I done to deserve this? What has she done to deserve this? I am not strong enough to handle this or bear up under this sort of pain. I need my mom still; I'm still grieving the loss of my brother. The timing is all wrong."*

And then, for whatever reason, I remember that second grader in the front seat of the bus, cowering in terror the first day the eighth-grade bully sat down next to her. As much as I crave days that are sunny and bright, there is a need for rain. The rain can be perceived as something dismal and unpleasant. It alters plans and gets me wet, but I desperately need it.

"How can this be, God, that You would allow all of this to happen, to my mom, and right now? Are you sure about this?" I sense God's gentle presence surrounding me. The raindrops fall, intermingling with my tears. I don't want this, don't want any of it,

but I need it. I need to be reminded of the fragility of life, of the things that should truly be my focus and priority, and of what (or more importantly Who) my faith rests on. Then a verse comes to mind: "I have told you these things, so that in me you may have peace. In this world you will have trouble. But take heart! I have overcome the world" (John 16:33).

I am not promised an easy life; far from it. Jesus suffered here on earth for me, and understands all that I am going through. He never promised to take away all the hardship, but He did promise to walk beside me through it and to help carry my burdens. He allows me to be pushed, sometimes far outside my comfort zone. He presents me with challenges and expects me to grow in my faith in the midst of them. *Will I trust Him?* That is the crux of the matter, the true test of faith. Will I trust Him even when it appears that my entire world is crumbling around me?

I have to respond, *"Yes! I don't understand, Lord, perhaps I never will, but yes, I do trust You. Though the rains may fall and my faith is pushed to the limit, I know You will never leave or forsake me."*

Mom and I orange picking in 2013

25. The Idea of Faith

A few years ago, my oldest son Carter was at a neighbor's house playing around with their miniature golf clubs. As soon as he got home, he wanted to try some more golf with Daddy. He was enthusiastic about it, but suddenly realized how much harder golf is than it might appear at first glance. Yes, some balls went soaring gracefully through the air from a perfect chip shot, but more often they went off to the side, didn't lift off the ground, moved an inch or two, or failed to make contact with his club altogether.

He soon realized that the "idea" of golf and how fun it could be was a whole lot easier than playing the real thing. It takes practice, patience, and time to learn, and doesn't happen in an afternoon. There will always be disappointing shots that don't go where we want them to, but we can't just quit. We have to keep playing the game.

The next night he was playing in the family room while we cleaned up after dinner and out of the blue asked my husband, "If you had to pick whether to worship an idol or get thrown into the fire, which would you pick?" They had read the story at bedtime of Shadrach, Meshach, and Abednego in Daniel 2 the week before and it was still on his mind. We tried to talk to him about it for a few minutes and explain how hard it is to believe and stand strong in your faith when someone is being tested like that.

"But if you said you wouldn't worship the idol, you wouldn't have to worry, God would always protect you," he responded. I wasn't sure what to say. I didn't know that it was the right time or age to be talking to him about how many millions of men and women have been martyred for their faith over the centuries. I would like to give my son a neat and tidy answer that God always protects those who believe in Him. We adults know that in a fallen world full of sin, this is not the case.

Faith is initially appealing to some because of the warm and fuzzy sense of God's love and forgiveness, and the reality of His care and concern for us. Then as soon as we are tested, we want to blame God and often turn from Him in hurt and distrust, feeling He has let us down so therefore we no longer owe Him our allegiance.

The "idea" of faith seems good and right to many, and many a person you ask would say they have some kind of faith. When that "good" concept is tested, then the rubber meets the road. Life is full of these reality checks. If we choose to quit the second we encounter adversity, we won't make it far in our pursuits and the same applies to faith.

Faith is not a feeling or some knowledge we acquire. Faith is a day-in and day-out relationship we have with God, realizing we will never know it all, never reach a full understanding of why things happen in our lives the way they do. Faith is also realizing that God loves us infinitely more than we could ever imagine and wants the very best for us.

I hope that my husband and I can gradually find a way to fully articulate this to my children because I don't want them to have a flawed view of faith and what it means for life. I want them to remember the words from John 16:33: "In this world you will have trouble." I want them to know that with faith comes hope, "and hope does not disappoint because the love of God has been poured out within our hearts through the Holy Spirit who was given to us" (Romans 5:5).

26. The Games We Play

I was following my daughter Sienna, who was two-years-old at the time, from room to room. She entered her own room, and immediately turned around and slammed the door in my face. It was nothing personal, she just liked the fact that she could do it. I opened the door to see what she was up to and she immediately screamed and pushed it shut again. I waited thirty seconds and peeked in again, and again she was right there, screaming at me and pushing it shut. This time I waited, all the while peeking through the crack under the door to see what she was doing.

She walked across the room to pick up a toy. Then I saw her feet, turning and walking back toward the door. Upon arriving back at the door, she realized she couldn't reach the door knob to open the door. Seconds later, I heard a meek little voice calling, "Mama, mama." I opened the door and she fell into my arms with a big smile on her face. She took for granted that I'd be right there, waiting for her to call, ready to step in and help her once she was ready to accept my help.

As I was sitting there holding my child, chuckling a little to myself at this game she plays, I immediately thought of a parallel. We do the very same thing all the time with God. We're on a path and we think we know exactly where we are going and what we need to do. We don't need any help and don't want any interference, especially from God. When He might try to show us a better way, we often slam the door in His face. "I don't want you, God. I don't want Your rules; I don't want You telling me what to do with my life." We choose a path and we are confident in the way we have chosen. Then, all of a sudden, we realize we're stuck. We need help, and where do we turn?

Our perspective of things sitting here on earth cannot compare to the perspective of Almighty God. How often do we look like that stubborn, silly little child who wants her own way until she realizes the consequences of slamming the door in her parent's face? People often complain that God is trying to restrict their freedom and confine them within many rules. What they fail to recognize is that He does this for their own good. What is more remarkable is that even when we slam that door again and again in God's face, He's always waiting, just around the corner, to pick us up and dust us off when we are ready to go to Him for help.

27. Have You Read the Instructions?

"I don't understand! What am I supposed to do?
This doesn't make any sense!"

I hear statements like this regularly from my children, and often my reply is simply, "Have you read the instructions?" Whether it's learning a new board game, working on a school assignment, or assembling a new toy, the kids often try to bypass the instructions and first try to figure it out on their own. After rolling their eyes or grumbling a time or two, they grudgingly accept my advice to read those instructions that always shed so much light on the problem.

Don't we all try to skip ahead and get straight to the "good stuff" without first reading the instructions? As I sat in a friend's family room, waiting for my daughter to finish a sewing lesson, I noticed a worn Bible nestled on a shelf under the coffee table. Clearly it had been read many, many times and was well-treasured by its owner.

Seeing that Bible struck me because I could suddenly see God saying to me, "When situations in your life don't make sense, when you are questioning the reason or timing of something, when you simply don't understand, have you first read the instructions? Have you been pouring over My word? Do you know My promises and really believe in and trust them?"

I remember my own grandmother's Bible. The cover was worn and tattered, the delicate pages creased, marked, and yellowed. That book was clearly an important part of her life, deeply cherished and consulted on a daily basis. Do I treat my Bible as an instruction manual for life? Do I dig into it looking for answers, realizing that those men and women of long ago were facing many problems exactly like my own?

How many times do I find myself praying for answers, feeling uncertain, discouraged, and confused, but failing to go first to the Word? When I do read the Word, God's intense love for me just pours out of the pages. I am struck that He gave me this amazing tool to get through life's most difficult trials, that He cared enough to do this for me! As I'm facing so many giants in my life, I wonder to myself, "How am I going to make it through this? What should I do? How do I handle so much heartache and discouragement?" His answer comes quietly and in the form of a tattered old book.

"Have you read the instructions today?"

Chapter 6
Hardship

I have a triangle scar on the palm of my right hand from a playground race back in the first grade. I was racing against a boy who clearly had the upper hand; he was taller, stronger and more athletic than I. I started out strong, but around the first corner, I slipped and fell, cutting my hand on the sharp edge of a railroad tie. Hand bleeding and confidence crushed, I decided I still had to finish strong. In an epic, Eric Liddell-like moment, I picked myself up and ran with all the gusto of an Olympic sprinter to win the race. I think my opponent had written me off the second I fell, and he slowed down significantly. The shock on his face as I passed him for the win was priceless.

I was picked on for being short, and began challenging all of my antagonists to race me each day at recess. My teacher actually refereed the races. She was rooting for me, applauding my efforts to diffuse a difficult situation in a constructive manner.

I must go through a similar proving ground in my faith walk. When I'm tested by trials or doubts, how will I respond? When times get tough, when answers don't come easily and situations seem not to make sense, will my faith hold up? I have discovered that hardship can do one of two things; it can either destroy a person or it can make him or her stronger. The scars that I have picked up along the way are proof of my ability to move on from a difficulty, to heal, and to continue through life. Each experience I have and lesson I learn make me stronger and better able to handle the next challenge. Had I not experienced smaller difficulties in my childhood and adolescence, the massive daily challenges I now face would certainly have overwhelmed me to the point of despair.

I can see it all fitting together more now, like a jigsaw puzzle that is beginning to take form. It doesn't all make sense yet; there are still many missing pieces and gaping holes. Hardship gives me the perseverance to encounter these holes and still trust in God's plan for me. Hardship drives me more toward God than any "good" times ever could. It makes every moment I spend with Him more precious, more life-sustaining, and more essential for my day-to-day survival.

28. Feet That Are Beautiful

Let my life today be an answer to someone else's
prayer. I am here for a purpose and that purpose
isn't just to focus on "me."

That's a good thought to start off the day, don't you think? Here is another one:

How, then, can they call on the one they have not believed in? And how can they believe in the one of whom they have not heard? And how can they hear without someone preaching to them? And how can anyone preach unless they are sent? As it is written: "How beautiful are the feet of those who bring good news!" (Romans 10:14-15)

Give me feet that are beautiful, today, oh God! I cry out for meaning and purpose in my days of sorrow, but it could be that my purpose is to share in this suffering with others who suffer, to encourage the downtrodden, and to exalt the name of my God in times of trial. Give me feet that are beautiful, feet that are strong to carry the message of hope You offer to this broken world. Give me a message, words to speak, and a heart that is focused on You, not on me. Someone is praying for help and relief right now. Someone is lost, hurting, in need of a friend, or sick. Let me be part of the answer.

Give me feet to carry the good news to others. Give me feet full of purpose each day to do Your will, and to serve others with great joy.

29. A Record of Our Lives

Have you ever experienced a personal drought, a time of difficulty? I love the imagery of rings on a tree stump. From the outside, a tree may appear rugged and healthy but inside that tree is the story and timeline of its development through the droughts, the scorching sun, and the harsh winters. What we behold is the strong exterior but there is more to that tree than what we see.

Drought may not be good for a tree, but can it be good for people? In the midst of it, I think everyone's answer would be a resounding no. Any suffering never appears to have a good purpose. I think most of us would readily admit, however, that if we didn't experience any hardship, we would only take the good times for granted. If we weren't ever sick, we wouldn't appreciate the times of health. If it never rained, we would grow to expect and ignore the days with beautiful sunshine. If there was never a time of tight finances, we would never appreciate the times of economic prosperity. A long, hard winter makes me eager for the first warm breezes and delicate flowers of spring.

Hardship causes us to brush aside all those distractions and things of little importance to focus on the things that really matter. Pain helps us reach down into the depths of our hearts and discover where our strength is rooted. I hope that I can someday look back over my life and pick out those times when there was suffering and pain and see how God was working behind the scenes to make me a stronger person through them. Rather than allowing myself to wallow in self-pity and doubt, I want to emerge a better person who is more aware than ever before of how blessed I truly am, in *so* many ways.

> Not only so, but we also glory in our sufferings, because we know that suffering produces perseverance; perseverance, character; and character, hope. And hope does not put us to shame, because God's love has been poured out into our hearts through the Holy Spirit, who has been given to us (Romans 5:3-5).

30. Layers

We started a tradition of making piñatas for our kids' birthday parties a number of years ago. I know they can be bought at the store, but there is just something special about a homemade piñata. These piñatas have been known to outlast the beating of a metal bat from 12 adolescent boys for almost 30 minutes. They have become a highlight of our kids' parties, and are worth every minute of extra effort. I woke up early one morning to do my devotions and work on the piñata. Crouched in the humid garage at 6:30 AM, applying strip after strip of sticky newspaper to the growing ball, I had to laugh. I was six layers down with four more to go by Saturday's party. I set the piñata outside to let it dry in the sun. Later that afternoon, after shopping for piñata "prizes," my daughter and I spread everything out on the kitchen table and I cut a small hole in the piñata. I admired the many layers of now-hardened newspaper that made up the shell.

Lawson and Sienna with their piñata

I saw a parallel then, that my life is a lot like a piñata and so is yours. We start out with only the thinnest shell of protection. Our life experiences are limited and we don't have much knowledge at all. With each milestone, experience, skill learned, and trial faced, a new layer is added. My faith has had to endure many experiences, tests, and trials to reach the point I'm at today. I'm certain there will be many more tests and layers yet to come.

This process of adding new layers is a long one. In order for the piñata to stay together properly, I can only add one layer at a time and I have to give it time to dry properly before adding another. I've tried to add a layer before the previous one is dry, which is not a good decision. After hours of work, I've had a piñata completely cave in because I tried to rush it.

Building a piñata is messy work too. The flour and water mixture has to be made just right – not too thick and heavy, and not too watery and thin. I have to plunge my hands right into it and not be afraid to get it all over me. Working on the piñata with my daughter helping resulted in not just messy hands, but sticky flour-water splashed all over our legs and clothing as well. In the same way, spiritual maturity can be a messy and difficult process. It can't be rushed or forced along. It is a slow and steady climb that lasts for the full measure of one's life.

I thought about building layers of faith and the strengthening that occurs when we are made weak. Those are times when we must allow God's word to soak into our hearts and souls and change our wayward spirits to conform to His will. A verse related to this concept is found in James 1:2-4 in *The Message* translation:

> Consider it a sheer gift, friends, when tests and challenges come at you from all sides. You know that under pressure, your faith-life is forced into the open and shows its true colors. So don't try to get out of anything prematurely. Let it do its work so you become mature and well-developed, not deficient in any way.

The piñata was ready for the birthday party and the kids took turns smashing it to bits as I watched with a satisfied smile on my face. My life journey is similar to the process it took to make that piñata. I'll always remember that my heavenly Father is watching over me, overseeing the often painful process (for me) of adding new layer upon new layer. I'll trust that these layers will all serve an important purpose, so that someday I can be "complete and not lacking anything."

31. Comfort and Joy

I know what it is to be in need, and I know
what it is to have plenty. I have learned the secret
of being content in any and every situation,
whether well fed or hungry, whether living in
plenty or in want. I can do everything through
Him who gives me strength
(Philippians 4:12-13).

Winter is the season that abounds with things that bring us relief from the elements. We enjoy crackling fires, cozy sweaters and blankets, mugs of hot cocoa, and evenings spent indoors in the company of family and friends. We sing familiar Christmas carols, many proclaiming messages of peace, joy, and love. We enjoy recreating our well-established and familiar traditions.

Life doesn't always allow us the luxury of staying in these places of familiarity. After the birth of our fifth child, I found myself in a state I affectionately call "the newborn haze." These are dreaded times for any parent when we operate on barely any sleep, spending more time awake at night than peacefully at rest. The days are long too and the demands incessant. In this place of nearly constant discomfort, how do I find joy? When life is less than comfortable, how can I still find contentment and peace? Does God see my struggles and really care about them? Does He have reasonable expectations of what I can truly handle?

My personal comfort isn't necessarily paramount on God's to-do list. As much as I'd like it to be, that just isn't the case. Just because I am in a place of difficulty I should not lose faith. God's infinite wisdom gives Him a perspective so much greater than mine. He is working, even in the midst of the most difficult days and times. He is shaping me into the person He wants me to be, in spite of and even through the difficult seasons. Therefore, my joy is not and should not be contingent on my comfort.

When I pause to soul-search, I realize it is always in the difficult times that I feel closest to God. I cry out to Him more, not when my days are breezing by easily, but when I'm gripping the narrow ledge of sanity by the very tips of my fingers. I can do *all things*. How many times have I heard this verse and paid little heed to its true meaning? I have joy in my heart today, not because my life has been easy or comfortable for the past few years.

I have joy because *I have God*.

32. The White House

When I was young, I can remember occasionally going to the mall with my mom. Every once in a while, we'd drive to a mall that was farther away and much larger. One store in particular stood out to me because it had almost a mystical quality. This particular store extended out and you could see everything it had on display through its glass displays and walls. What's more, everything in the store was white. I had never seen anything like it. Sometimes we would walk through, looking at the clothes. Who, I wondered, wore these beautiful all-white clothes?

Nowadays, White House is combined with Black Market, which is much more practical in my opinion, being the fashion expert that I am. Maybe it's just that I'm a mother of five and don't own any white clothes anymore. The last white shirt I owned was ruined when someone used my shoulder to clean off their choco-late-covered face. My life is much too messy for white.

If I waited to come to the Lord until I got my life in order, I'd never make it. It's about as futile as me trying to keep my house clean or clothes white. As soon as I finish cleaning a room, the kids are messing it up again. I can't blame all my messiness on them for I've got my own flaws that crop up again and again. I've got my issues that look like dark stains on a once-white garment.

Sometimes, I get to the end of a day in utter discourage-ment. I've started out the day with a plan in mind for how I'd like things to go, but by the end it feels like absolutely nothing has gone the way I planned. I haven't even been able to carve out a few quiet minutes to pray, thinking *how can I walk into His presence looking like this? I'm a shabby mess!* Sometimes approaching God in this less-than-perfect state feels a lot like walking into the White House. I don't really belong there, but when I make the time to enter, He meets me at the door with a smile and warm welcome. His perfection overshadows all my imperfections and shortcomings. He washes me whiter than snow:

> Purge me with hyssop, and I shall be clean; Wash me, and I shall be whiter than snow. (Psalm 51:7 NKJV)

I wish I could spend every day in the White House, feeling serene and clean and perfect. In reality, I am on the battlefield of life, elbows-deep in dirt and grime. I've questioned God far too many times about being this way. Why must life be so hard and messy? Why can't every story have a happy ending? Why does there have to be so much pain?

His answer comes in the quiet of the early morning hours. He reminds me I'm not in the White House and things here will never be easy or pain-free. That's the nature of living in a sin-stained world and also the reason I put my hope, not in the here and now, but in Him and in my eternal future. I will look forward to wearing those garments of pure white someday.

33. Unrealized Potential

He straps on shin guards, puts on his cleats, and races out the door, eager to play soccer in the backyard. He grits his teeth and kicks the ball again and again with great determination and as much strength as he can muster. Beads of perspiration begin to form on his little forehead and he races back across the yard to grab his sippy cup, taking giant gulps of water before running back to play some more.

My son Lawson has all the passion and drive of a professional soccer player. What he lacks is size and maturity. Until he has time to grow, to gain life experience and be tested on the field, his skills will be weak and incomplete. Until he develops discipline, he will not become a great soccer player.

If I'm striving to be a runner, I will never realize my full potential by sitting on the couch all day. If I'm aspiring to be a great chef, I'll never amount to anything by ordering takeout for all my meals. The same is true in the Christian walk. If I want to grow in my faith and be closer to God, become more mature and be fruitful, I've got to push myself, reprioritize, and be tested.

> God, your God, is testing you to find out if you totally love him with everything you have in you. You are to follow only God, your God, hold Him in deep reverence, keep His commandments, listen obediently to what He says, serve Him—hold on to Him for dear life! (Deuteronomy 13:3-4 MSG).

Testing is a healthy and necessary part of life. Testing reveals true character, gives cause to reevaluate priorities, causes us to appreciate our blessings. Testing brings us to a deeper place in our faith than we could reach by any other means.

I am truly a work in progress and so are you. We have much unrealized potential, and I know that in these days of trial and pain, God is working to develop that potential. He's chipping away at the old to reveal something so much better in me. During the summer months, my kids and I watch Monarch caterpillars growing and shedding their skins to make room for their rapidly growing bodies. I recognize that I too am growing, and that I need to shed off my former sins to make way for the newness I find in the Lord. Only then can He do a good work in me, and can I begin to become who He wants me to be.

Chapter 7
A Plan Much Greater than Mine

I love to draw and took art lessons for several years when I was young. I remember toting all my art supplies and a new drawing pad to class, eager to begin a new masterpiece. You can imagine my frustration and disappointment when I soon realized that my instructor had no intention of allowing me to dive in and draw my masterpiece on the first day of class. First, I had to set the stage for what was to come. I had to measure out the placement of my image on the page. I had to make light sketches of where it would start and some basic shapes that would be the framework for the actual picture. The process was difficult, abstract, and it was not fun. I would close my notebook after the hour-long class and feel like I had nothing to show for it. I knew that I could have drawn something great, if she would just let me. Why all this boring planning? I would have to wait another full week to continue work on my picture.

As I went through this process again and again, however, I began to understand it more. I learned that it was a necessary part of art, for then the picture was more precise, well-proportioned, and more accurately portrayed on my paper when I took the time to perform these extra steps at the beginning.

Similarly, I've witnessed God's hand in my life, setting the stage for things to come. If I view certain events and responses to my prayers in isolation, I can become confused or discouraged. I must trust His preparatory steps for He has a plan much greater than any I could ever imagine. I must have faith that He is working behind the scenes, orchestrating the events just like my art teacher had me orchestrate my sketches. Even when I can't see the bigger picture, I won't be robbed of my joy. I will watch with great hope and expectation as His masterpiece unfolds in my life.

34. The Whole Story

I was sitting in the family room with two of the children reading books. My daughter, Sienna, eagerly ran to the bookshelf to grab a few selections. The kids' older cousins had just given us some hand-me-down books and one of them was a 150-page volume about George Washington (clearly not two-and-half-year-old material). I gently told her, "You are too little for this book." "No, Mama," she adamantly proclaimed, "read it!"

"No." I tried to explain again, "this book is too long for you." "Read it, Mama! Read it!" We went back and forth like this for a couple of minutes, and I could not convince her otherwise. I started to flip through the book and every once in a while there was a black and white picture with a small caption. I read a couple of those captions to her, and quickly enough she lost interest and turned to a Dr. Seuss book that was more up her alley. And as I was setting the George Washington book aside, the thought suddenly hit me that this was the same conversation I had been having with God all week.

Losing my brother at such a young age has tested my faith to the core. I have been asking God again and again, "Why? Give me some reason for this, God. Can't you explain to me the 'story' that is playing out here? This just doesn't seem right." God, lovingly and patiently, was looking down on me saying, "Oh Shelley, what you ask of Me is not something for you to know right now. I can't reveal the whole story to you. This is a story far too complex and detailed, far too intense for your human mind to grasp. But this you must know. I am in control. I love you, and even when everything seems to be going wrong, you can still (and always) put your hope in me."

God gives us a piece of the story in the Bible. He lovingly placed these words together for us as a guidebook to follow, but He never implies that we will receive all the answers to all our questions. He requires us to trust Him. All my life, God has used these trying moments to bring me to a new level of faith. Again and again, I have seen His hand working during the times when I was tempted to throw up my hands in defeat and despair.

God is the Author of our faith. He has a perfect plan in everything. My finite human mind cannot begin to comprehend what He has in store for me or how He might possibly use the trials in my life or the lives of others. He can't always give us the answers or the outcomes we wish for, and a big part of faith requires us to trust Him, even when nothing makes sense and when the story seems to be all wrong. God has taught me to share His love with others, to be bold in my faith despite my human doubts and struggles to understand, and to wait on Him for understanding when everything seems to be turned upside-down.

35. Ever Seeing but Never Perceiving

He told them, "The secret of the kingdom of
God has been given to you. But to those on the
outside everything is said in parables so that,
'they may be ever seeing but never perceiving,
and ever hearing but never understanding;
otherwise they might turn and be forgiven!'"
(Mark 4:11-12).

My daughter Sienna, who was two at the time, wanted to have some candy one morning. She got her candy bin out and brought it over to me, asking, "Can I have some candy?" I promptly told her she could not for it was only 9 AM. She asked again, and again I said no, but this time I told her, "It's not good for your tummy." She asked again, and I told her she needed to wait until later. She asked again, and I tried to go into the digestive complications that could result if she had a diet mainly consisting of candy. She immediately asked, "Can I have some candy?"

No matter what I told her, she was clearly, absolutely, positively not going to listen to anything I said that didn't result in her getting the candy. Clearly she knew I was saying no to her every time but was stubbornly refusing to accept that answer. She understood the reality, but refused to accept it.

As she was "helping" me clean the bathroom a little later, which for her means sitting on the counter and smearing water all over the mirror, I was thinking about her stubborn persistence with a little smile on my face. No matter what I said to her or how I explained it, she wasn't having my answer about the candy first thing in the morning.

Something clicked in me because suddenly the concept of a hardened heart made a lot more sense. God gives clear guidelines and truths to us, and we also are given the free will to either accept those or reject them. He knows our hearts and He isn't interested in persuading us by all means to accept his Word. He gives us the truth, and it's up to us to accept or reject it.

Truth is always the truth. It seems obvious that no one should have a steady diet of candy, and that no matter how much we want it, it's not a good idea. In the same way, we try to bargain with God all the time for things we think we want or we think are good for us, when in reality they really aren't. We try to justify behavior based on what is best for us, not necessarily what is right or true. The truth is staring us in the face, but we harden our hearts to it and try to work around it any way we can.

When I am caught up in the vortex of mothering young children, it is often tempting to use my busy schedule or my fatigue as excuses for not listening to and obeying God. I may be tempted to think, "I just don't have anything left to give, God!!" This too can be a form of hardening our hearts if we let it.

When God gives clear commands to "love your enemies," "bless those who curse you," "give to those in need," "let your light shine before men," "do unto others," forgive, serve, share, sacrifice, encourage, or pray, He doesn't provide a footnote with a list of exemptions.

36. Whiter than Snow

"Come now, let us settle the matter," says the Lord.
"Though your sins are like scarlet, they
shall be as white as snow; though they are red as
crimson, they shall be like wool" (Isaiah 1:18).

I awoke to a gorgeous scene, the yard completely blanketed in a layer of perfect, fluffy white snow. What a calming effect it had to see everything covered in white. It brought a new appreciation for each tiny twig on every tree when it has those sparkly white flakes resting on it. What seemed dreary and unattractive just the day before was transformed into a glorious glittering masterpiece! Of course, then my kiddos awoke and there was a flurry of winter coats and mittens as they prepared to go outside. They skipped breakfast in favor of several hours of outdoor play in the winter wonderland and soon that winter wonderland was a

Carter and Sienna sledding in the backyard

maze of footprints and grass where snow had been removed. My picture-perfect backyard was gone.

I love the transforming aspect of snow, how it instantly makes something unattractive seem brighter, cleaner, and more beautiful. I was reminded while looking out at the sparkling white snow of a verse from Isaiah that demonstrates how God transforms us in our sinfulness. He makes us as white as snow. There is a reason He chose that analogy, for it is a powerful one. When snow falls to the earth, it blankets everything evenly. It shows no favoritism wherever it lands.

God extends His offer of forgiveness to us in this same manner. And when God is at work in our lives, we can be sure He is making a masterpiece. He can take any mess and clean it up again. No sin is too great for Him to forgive. He promises us, "Behold I am making all things new!" (Revelation 21:5). No matter how ugly our lives become, He offers us renewal and restoration. He cleanses us completely.

When I awaken in the morning to a coating of newly-fallen snow, I will recall this miracle of forgiveness. I will rejoice in a God who revels in the details, who uses millions of tiny crystals of ice to paint a visual display of the beauty and glory of forgiven sins and a fresh start in our once-fallen lives.

37. Turkeys and True Dependence

"Did you know you have a turkey in your backyard?"

Well yes, I actually did notice that. "Yes," I told our little neighbor who had come by after dinner to share this news. About four days earlier, our newest feathered friend, who my daughter Sienna affectionately named Toots, showed up to dine under our bird feeders. She appeared at least once or twice a day for many days after that. Another beautiful bird arrived shortly thereafter as a lovely Mother's Day surprise, the Rose-Breasted Grosbeak, one of my favorites.

I never cease to be amazed by the beauty and diversity of God's creation that covers the gamut from the gangling, awkward turkey to the astonishingly beautiful grosbeak. Both are different and marvelous to behold. I welcome these glimpses of beauty in my often-chaotic and messy world. They are reminders of the bigger picture of what is unfolding beyond these four walls for most of my waking hours.

There seems a dissonance at times between the beauty of the world around me and the pain and trouble I see in my own life. I long for harmony and order and when they don't come, I struggle to understand. God often uses pain in our lives to bring us closer to Him, and as I consider this truth, I realize that in order to be close to God, we first have to need Him.

But wait, don't I know this? I've been following Him for as long as I can remember, haven't I? Yes, but I'm as susceptible to the human condition of "self" as anyone else. I have no need for the down-on-my-knees prayers of a desperate person when things are going smoothly: "If I must boast, I will boast of the things that show my weakness" (2 Corinthians 11:30).

Paul was imprisoned when he wrote several of his greatest books of the Bible. He understood the human tendency to rely on one's own strength. He went so far as to say he would boast of his weaknesses. He penned the words, "When I am weak, then I am strong" and I can truly understand now why he would have written such a thing. I'm so much better off when I'm in true dependence on God than when I'm trying to stumble my way through life on my own. Sometimes things happen that are unexpected and confusing. He's calling me, at those times more than any other, to simply trust and know that He is still in control.

38. Growth Spurt

My son Carter came up to me the other day with a funny little limp in his walk. He stopped when he got to me, looked down at his feet, and said, "I think my shoes are too small." Sure enough, as I looked down, I could see where his big toes were bulging out in the front of his shoes, trying to make room where there wasn't any. Just when I think I'm set with all the kids' clothes, it never fails that someone grows out of something!

Growth isn't an easy process. It keeps us in a constant state of change and uncertainty. It doesn't happen at a steady and predictable pace. We have no control over it – its amount or timing.

I often find myself reminiscing about the past. A pleasant image or memory comes to mind and I long to return to that time in my life. Somehow, I seem to think that things were easier back then. It is hard not to be wooed by those whispers of the past, craving them instead of my present reality. But that past is just that – the past – and is not God's will for me.

Growth is painful, uncomfortable, and awkward. It propels me toward an unfamiliar place called the unknown. Philippians 3:7-14 in the NIV translation beautifully addresses the pain and triumph of growing gracefully.

> But whatever were gains to me I now consider loss for the sake of Christ. What is more, I consider everything a loss because of the surpassing worth of knowing Christ Jesus my Lord, for whose sake I have lost all things. I consider them garbage, that I may gain Christ and be found in him, not having a righteousness of my own that comes from the law, but that which is through faith in Christ—the righteousness that comes from God on the basis of faith. I want to know Christ—yes, to know the power of his resurrection and participation in his sufferings, becoming like him in his death, and so, somehow, attaining to the resurrection from the dead.

> Not that I have already obtained all this, or have already arrived at my goal, but I press on to take hold of that for which Christ Jesus took hold of me. Brothers and sisters, I do not consider myself yet to have taken hold of it. But one thing I do: Forgetting what is behind and straining toward what is ahead, I press on toward the goal to win the prize for which God has called me heavenward in Christ Jesus.

The future scares me at times. I will have to let go of so many things, so many comforts that are around me today in order to move into it. The race course is set out for me, but will I run it? I cannot go backwards – I can only move forward. I'll have to shed those ill-fitting shoes and in faith venture out in a new and untested pair, breaking them in as I walk. I must press on for hope lies in the future as God's plans for me unfold and are fulfilled.

39. Things that Get in the Way

"The Lord will give [unyielding and
impenetrable] strength to His people;
the Lord will bless His people with peace"
(Psalm 29:11 AMPC).

It's easy to focus on obstacles that get in our way as we walk through life. They thwart our plans and confuse us. We can see the way but the road is cluttered with debris. It's even tempting at times to throw in the towel and give up. We look at these barriers from our limited human perspective, and conclude that we cannot handle what we encounter.

I was thinking over this verse from Psalm 29 one day while observing my son Carter's soccer game. He fired off a couple of tricky kicks to get around defenders and past the goalie, and this was such a great visual reminder of my need to overcome obstacles in my own path.

A sense of fear is often what accompanies burdens that seem too heavy, and obstacles that seem insurmountable – the fear of being trapped, fear of thinking things will never get better, fear of failure, and fear of the unknown. Too often I let overwhelming obstacles cloud my vision of what God is capable of doing.

I try rather than trust.

Faith isn't just believing in God; it's the ability to trust in Him even when our circumstances seem to be swallowing us alive. Faith bypasses all human capabilities and places the full responsibility for the outcome on God. We are promised in Psalm 55:22, "Cast your burden on the Lord, and He shall sustain you" and in Matthew 11:28, "Come to me, all you who are weary and burdened, and I will give you rest."

I will not always be able to work around, overcome, or have the strength to combat things that get in the way of my faith and mar my peace. That makes me ever so glad I know the One who can!

40. Fairness and Faith

It took great grit and determination (and several changes of gloves) on this wet, blustery morning, for my daughters Reese and Sienna to roll and smash together a small snowman. It was not the best snowman they ever made or the prettiest, but the effort that went into building it made it all the more special, and made the achievement all the more noteworthy. It took much time while they endured the cold, but the result was well worth it. They were undeterred by the lack of the basic element of a snowman, which

Reese's and Sienna's snowman

is snow. They could have given up, but they didn't. They had faith that their efforts would be rewarded with success, and they were.

God does not dole out blessings in equal measure. We go through seasons where life is hard, and seasons where things seem to go our way. While some are basking in financial security and wealth, others are barely scraping by. While some are blessed with great health, others are battling illnesses. While some seem to avoid tragedy and difficulty, others are immersed in it regularly. It may seem as though the pressures bear down relentlessly, and it is tempting to think that life is not fair.

Some think that having a belief in God somehow entitles us to an easier life, that the minute we decide to follow Him, our road will become less bumpy, our relationships will become less complicated, and our worries will fade away. We brashly come before God with expectations of what He can and should do for us, and He ever-so-gently reminds us through His ever-present grace that He ultimately knows what is best and fair, and what we truly need.

One morning as we drove to church, I was reminded of George Mueller, a man who regularly demonstrated his faith publicly. While he should have been receiving bountiful blessings for his steadfast work with orphans, he was constantly in a position of relying solely on God's provision for their most basic needs. When they literally had nothing to eat or drink, he prayed a prayer of thanksgiving, with all the children seated at the table, and the food and milk showed up. He could have given up hope many times, but he did not lose faith. He could have become bitter that God continued to test his faith over and over again, but he didn't.

He recognized something that many of us fail to discover about faith: *It is meant to be tested. This is the key concept for His work to be accomplished in us.* God doesn't want us to be confidently striding through life, but rather down on our knees in a posture of prayer: "Always be joyful. Never stop praying. Be thankful in all circumstances, for this is God's will for you who belong to Christ Jesus" (1 Thessalonians 5:16-18 NLT).

41. The Green Ribbon

"There is a time for everything . . . a season for everything under the sun . . . ." (Ecclesiastes 3:1).

I glanced out the window with dismay as my daughter Sienna marched into the room. Yes, there was still snow on the ground and a blustery wind was blowing. She put on her sandals and said, "I'm ready."

"Oh, sweetheart, you can't wear that today. It's freezing cold out!"

She looked down at her pretty pink leotard, but was not ready to concede her choice of wardrobe. After much coaxing, coercing, and threats of losing dessert for a day, week, or the rest of her life, I got her to put on some pants and a jacket and we made our way out to the car. By then, I had managed to move her 15 feet in the right direction but it took 15 minutes. My challenges with her, however, were not finished.

"I don't want to ride in that car seat," she pronounced and I thought, *Oh for goodness sake, is this really something worth fighting over?* There is a time to laugh and a time to cry, and right about then I felt more like crying. *Wasn't the motivation of a fun gymnastics class enough to motivate her?*

"But today is the day you will get your ribbon at the end of class." She paused to think it over.

"But I wanted a pink ribbon, not a green one. I don't want that ribbon!" (She had found out ahead of time the color of this session's ribbon since my older daughter had already received hers the previous week.)

"You don't want your special ribbon?" I asked her incredulously. "Won't you be sad if you don't get your ribbon?"

Without a second of hesitation, she shot back, "No, it's not pink!" So much for giving thanks in *all* circumstances.

How often do we stubbornly turn our noses up at the things we ought to be thankful for? How often do we whine and complain and take for granted some of the greatest blessings in our lives? There are always things in my life, many things as a matter of fact, to be thankful for. How often do I sound just like my daughter as I react to things that happen in my life? How often am I stubbornly insisting on my way, even when everything points me in another direction?

From my limited human perspective, it is easy to look at a situation and whine, "Why God? This isn't the way things are supposed to be. Can't you fix this, change that, heal this person, or make this situation right again? I didn't sign up for the 'green ribbon.' I don't want it!"

My daughter did end up accepting her ribbon prize at the end of her class. She stood up, holding it proudly over her head with a big smile on her face. May we all take a few minutes to dwell on the blessings in our lives. May we accept, with grace and dignity, the challenges we face and the rewards we receive. In whatever season of life you find yourself today, God is there. In whatever trial, test, or deviation from "the plan," you can rest assured that He has a master plan, so much greater than we could ever imagine.

Chapter 8

A Gracious and Loving Father

As soon as his feet hit the ground, he was off and running. Where was he going? Who knows! I'm pretty sure even he didn't have a clue. He got a taste of freedom and that was all it took. I sighed as he rounded the corner of the house, running out of view, no doubt headed toward the street. Will he never tire of this game? Doesn't he realize all the toys and playmates are in the backyard? There is nothing for him in the front yard except the steep driveway and dangerous street.

I run toward my son, Lawson, loving him so much, despite his disobedience. I scoop him up into the safety of my arms and return him to the backyard. Sometimes he struggles, sometimes he accepts it. Sometimes he stays there for a few minutes, at other times he immediately turns around just to repeat the whole scenario all over again. One friend who witnessed his shenanigans told me with a chuckle, "You've got a runner there!" Indeed I do.

This morning as I woke up, I had a vision in my mind. I could see my dear son running away from me towards the front yard. I'm a runner too (no not the marathon kind) and if I'm honest, I've got a will just as stubborn as my toddler. I get a big whiff of freedom and I'm off running toward the street, turning my back on God. I get caught up in the day-to-day stuff that crowds Him out, I feel confident in my assessment of which places are "safe," walking away from His comforting rod and staff and leaving the safety of His pastures for the places where I think the grass looks greener.

He loves me, in spite of my running. How many times have I made Him sigh as I make the same mistakes over and over again? How often has He whispered to me, "Don't run away. Stay here in the safety of My arms." My heart wanders and loses focus of what is truly important because I think I know what is best. Clearly I don't. I'm thankful for the reminder of my tendency to run, and I'm speechless when I dwell on the full weight of this. I'm tired after chasing my son for just a few minutes. God has been dealing with this kind of behavior from me for my entire life. I haven't grown out of it after all these years, and He still chases after me.

42. Grace – Period

"Sienna colored the dresser with lip balm!" Those were not the words I wanted to hear as I was visiting with a friend and trying unsuccessfully to eat my lunch. The lip balm in question wasn't an old, half-used tube of ChapStick. It was a new EOS organic lip balm ball and those last a long time. I sucked a large gulp of air into my lungs when I saw the entire surface of the girls' dresser colored in the sticky lip balm.

I handed my daughter a container of wet wipes and told her to go clean it up. When she returned, I asked her, "Did you know that was a bad thing to do?" She nodded her head that she did. "Then why did you do it?" All I got back was a blank stare.

She sweetly asked me, "Since I did a good job cleaning it up, can I have ice cream now?" Wait, are you kidding me? This girl knows how to work the system! I told her that she didn't get a reward for fixing something she had messed up in the first place. I'm pretty sure that didn't register with her, but maybe someday she'll understand. Maybe.

As I was tucking her into bed that night, I sang her the same two songs I sing every night. Her eyes began to droop as she snuggled into her pillow, peaceful at last. This daughter has been a true test of my parenting skills, patience, and ability to stay calm and carry on. In spite of her daily agenda to push me over the edge, I love her. Sitting in the dimly-lit quiet of her room, I realized how similar her lobbying for a treat was to what I do all the time.

I've made a mess of things, and then done my best to clean it up, feeling pretty good about myself. I then think I have the right to ask God for a reward. More importantly, I realized how similar I am to her, and how I depend fully on the daily grace of God to forgive me for my mess-ups. Grace is an amazing, often-overlooked thing. Grace is *everything*.

This kind of self-reflection makes me thankful that my kids show me almost every day some aspect of my own character that needs work. They show me how great my need is for God and His forgiveness, love, and all-encompassing grace.

43. Granter of Requests

"I want this. Give me that. I need more. Help me with this." These are phrases I hear many times, every day. Sometimes, I'm able to tune them out or reply with calm answers. At other times, they get the best of me and I holler back, "Can't you wait?" or "Go get it yourself!" or "Not right now." Sometimes I feel like I'm just here to grant the kids their every wish and whim. I don't always handle very well the constant stream of requests or the reactions I receive when my kids don't get what they want at exactly the moment they want it. Wait? I don't want to wait. I want it right now! That is often my attitude and perhaps it's yours too.

Sometimes, we do have to wait. No one likes waiting. It can be difficult, painstaking, and frustrating. In my prayer life, I have a difficult time waiting for answers. I repeatedly ask and expect, wish for, and demand an immediate answer. I also want the answer I'm hoping for, that God would heal this person, help that person with a personal struggle, heal this relationship, or keep my kids healthy. The healing doesn't always come and the struggle isn't always removed. I go to the Granter of requests, but my requests aren't always granted in the way I desired. I want an easy answer, but I don't always want to expend any effort that requires patience, perseverance, and down-on-my-knees prayer.

We found and stored a chrysalis in our garage for six months from fall till spring. One April day, a beautiful butterfly emerged. To me, it was a miraculous moment when that ugly brown chrysalis broke open to reveal a delicate Swallowtail butterfly. The kids each got a minute to hold it before it took flight. What a special moment!

The periods of time when I wait for an answer to my prayer remind me of that chrysalis. Perhaps God is working, crafting a miracle under the surface of what appears to be ugly and lifeless. Perhaps what is coming is well worth the wait, and will far exceed what I could ever imagine. I bring my petitions to the Granter of requests and then I must wait. I trust that a God, who can design something as perfect as a butterfly will hear me and answer in His perfect time.

44. Stay Close

The car door opens and he darts out into the parking lot. Despite my desperate cries of "Wait, stay close to me!" he runs ahead, out into the path of great danger. Two-year-old Lawson bounds across the pavement with no concept of the danger he is in. I scream his name to come back, but he never even turns to look. Finally, he reaches the safety of the sidewalk. I sigh in relief and watch him turn to see where I am. Why doesn't he listen? He must know how much I love him, must know I'm looking out for him and want him to be safe? He must know I would throw myself in front of a car to save him?

I tuck him in at night, tenderly stroking his little face, the scenes from the day replaying in my mind. How strangely similar is this parking lot scenario to the relationship so many of us have with God? The freedom gets to our heads, so we turn from Him and run. Many never look back and life beats them up. They are run over by devastating circumstances and blame God for their predicament, even though He was there all along. He desires that we stay close beside Him, offering us protection from harm. "Stay close to Me," He calls. *Stay close*, in the good times and the bad.

Stay close...even when you think you know where you're going, what you're doing, what you need. *Stay close* to the One who loves you in the most extreme and phenomenal ways you could ever grasp.

45. Dependency

It's just another typical morning in the Berad home as I hear little feet rushing down the hall, tiny voices beckoning me out of my warm bed to begin another long and exhausting day. There are meals to be made, laundry to be done, diapers to change, school lessons to teach, errands to run, and rooms to clean. When I look at my kids, I see so much dependency and so many needs to be met. There is much time, energy, and care needed to get them through the day.

There are days, I'll readily admit it, that I daydream of a time when my house will be quiet again. I imagine what it will be like to wake up in the morning and be able to care for my own needs first, not the demanding needs of so many children.

In thinking about dependency, I compare my role as a parent to my relationship with God and how it is the complete opposite. He desires that I be fully dependent on Him for my entire life. He keeps me close and cherishes me and has even written my name on His own hands: "See I have engraved you on the palms of My hands" (Isaiah 49:16).

He knows our weaknesses and shortcomings all too well. He is familiar with our flaws and our inability to live life "on our own." He desires spiritual growth, expecting that we will mature and deepen in our faith over time, but we must train ourselves to keep coming back to Him for the very willpower we need to progress in our faith.

While I would never go so far as to cut ties with my children, I do want them to be self-sufficient one day. I would never train them to "need" me forever. No, my role is to teach them to depend on the One who can truly supply all their needs. No human can ever fulfill that role, only God can, as the psalmist reminded us: "Teach me your way, Lord, that I may rely on your faithfulness; give me an undivided heart, that I may fear your name" (Psalm 86:11).

What draws me away from God? There are many things. How can I truly have an "undivided heart," not letting the many distractions around me crowd Him out in my day-to-day living? I must depend on Him, recognizing my human tendencies to be self-sufficient and self-reliant, and to do all my problem-solving on my own.

It's not part of my natural inclination to be that dependent, It's a need I have to recognize and accept again and again.

Lord, instill in me a desire today to depend more on You and less on my own strength. Remind me how much I need You and supply me with all that I need for whatever purposes You have intended for me to accomplish here and now. Amen.

46. Carried

We are all born with an innate desire and need to be held closely and carried. As tiny infants, we are completely helpless. It is not just a need for transport but a necessity for development. We can't do anything for ourselves and are fully dependent on our caretakers to hold, nourish, clothe, care for, and protect us. Many times, a baby will crave just being held. There is scientific evidence that points to the importance of skin-to-skin contact between a newborn baby and its mother immediately after birth. Often when a baby cries, it is comforted almost immediately by the simple act of being held.

There is such great comfort in being held, in knowing we are safe and secure, that someone is looking out for us and won't let any harm come to us. But as we grow, we begin to take those first few steps on our own and we become addicted to the power of independence. We want to be held less and less as we gain confidence in our ability to move forward on our own.

When a child falls and scrapes his knee or bumps her head, the one thing that often soothes the accompanying tears is to be swept up in the loving arms of a parent. My little ones are growing heavier by the day. My arms and back ache after I've been carrying them around for even a short time, and they are quick to push me away when they feel they don't need me anymore.

We think we are strong and smart, and feel justified in our self-sufficiency. Then all of a sudden our securities come crashing down. Disaster strikes in the form of an illness, loss of a job, a crumbling marriage, financial trouble, depression, loss of a loved one, or anything that is out of our human control. We realize in that moment how fragile our lives truly are, how quickly all our securities can be toppled. It often takes that trial to bring us back to God. The faithful Father is waiting in the wings with arms open wide, ready to walk alongside us or even to pick us up if we'll only let Him.

No matter how far we've made it on our life journey, no matter how long we've been walking alone, our weight and our problems are never too heavy for God to carry. He will never turn us away!

I could never understand that kind of all-encompassing, never-failing love until I had children of my own. Now I cannot imagine turning my back on one of my precious children in their moment of need, and the same is true with God. I can rest assured in His love for me. I found a verse recently that painted a beautiful picture in my mind of God carrying me in Deuteronomy 33:12: "Let the beloved of the Lord rest secure in Him for He shields him all day long. And the one the Lord loves rests between his shoulders." I love the image of being carried by God, and not just carried, but placed over His shoulders.

47. Peace and Quiet

I wandered into the front yard for a few moments of peace. The kids were excitedly screaming as they all jumped on our big trampoline, and I needed a few quiet moments at the end of another long day, just to reflect and get my wits about me before the bedtime rush.

As I watered some of my flowers that were wilting from another hot and dry day, I noticed a number of large weeds growing in my flower beds. How do weeds always seem to sprout up so quickly? I grabbed hold of one of the offending weeds and pulled with all my might. It did not loosen as easily as I had hoped so I grasped it again with both hands, closer to the root and gave it a long, steady tug. Slowly, bit by bit, I could feel it giving way to my effort. I was amazed when I saw how long the roots were and discovered why the weeds were thriving while my grass withered in the summer heat.

I crave peace and a steady and reliable calm in my life. Why is it that the weeds are always waiting to crowd out what I desire most? Just like my flower beds, it seems there are not many days that things go as planned or as I would like. The kids fight, the house is a wreck, and my to-do list grows ever longer. If that isn't enough, I am haunted by the losses I've experienced in my family. I hang on with all my might, but the things that I love still slip away. I battle against the encroaching weeds, occasionally pulling one out by the roots, yet they continue to reappear.

Though the hot sun threatens to scorch my resolve and the foundations of faith, I hold fast to the promises God has provided for me. I realize that when I am rooted in Him, nothing can shake me, and no power can come against me and prevail. Even with the steady and constant din of this world, in Him I find such amazing peace and quiet.

I pray that from His glorious, unlimited resources He will empower you with inner strength through His Spirit. Then Christ will make His home in your hearts as you trust in Him. Your roots will grow down into God's love and keep you strong. And may you have the power to understand, as all God's people should, how wide, how long, how high, and how deep His love is. May you experience the love of Christ, though it is too great to understand fully. Then you will be made complete with all the fullness of life and power that comes from God (Ephesians 3:16-19 NLT).

48. Living in Auto

There aren't a lot of things we splurge on, but photography is a bit of a passion for me, so I own a decent camera. I love to take pictures because they are a great way to preserve our memories. When I'm having a bad day, I look back on them and they always help me keep things in perspective and brighten my mood. The one drawback with my camera, if I can call it that, is that I don't take full advantage of the many functions and capabilities it has to offer. Truth be told, I barely know how to use it! I've tried to watch tutorials and research tips online. I've even tried reading the manual. After all that, I still keep the dial mostly on the auto function and rely on my "smart" camera to make up for my lack of photo-taking ability.

I feel like my life can be that way too – living it on the auto setting all the time, which means I am not living it to its fullest potential. It's easy to let "the schedule" or "the to-do list" dictate my life and how my days pass and not really take advantage of all that is available to me. I'm living life out of focus most days and don't tap in to all the features and functionalities God has given me. I'm operating in one mode, that's the mode of me, by not venturing out into the great unknown of trust, surrender, and submission to Him.

I took my oldest daughter to a gymnastics meet once at the University of Pittsburgh. She had been involved in gymnastics for several years and absolutely loved it, but she had never really seen a real gymnastics competition to understand the outcome of years of practice. She had a surface understanding of gymnastics from her lessons, but didn't know what it looked like when someone was performing to their full potential. She sat there, watching in awe, as the girls flipped, spun, leaped, and swung. Each event was thrilling for her and she could hardly believe the kinds of tricks they were doing on apparati she had been working on for several years. "I could never do that" she said more than once.

Whether it's using a camera or doing complex gymnastics routines, we'll never function at our full potential if we don't push ourselves to move past the basics, get outside our comfort zones, practice, apply ourselves, and learn by making some mistakes. It's truly exhilarating when I suddenly realized that all I have seen thus far is only a taste of what is really out there. When I think about my Christian walk, getting out of auto means surrendering my will and comfort to accept direction from God. It means allowing Him to take the reins and give me a new perspective on life and how I should be living it. He helps me focus on the things that are truly important. He gives me the clearest image of what life is all about and what I'm ultimately working toward.

> Yet the Lord longs to be gracious to you; therefore he will rise up to show you compassion. For the Lord is a God of justice. Blessed are all who wait for him! People of Zion, who live in Jerusalem, you will weep no more. How gracious he will be when you cry for help! As soon as he hears, he will answer you... Whether you turn to the right or to the left, your ears will hear a voice behind you, saying, "This is the way; walk in it" (Isaiah 30:18-19, 21).

Chapter 9

Where Does My Help Come From?

He was insistent about doing it on his own. His pudgy little hands were swathed in too-large mittens where his thumbs could not fit into the thumb holes, but he did not hesitate for one second. He grabbed the handle of the heavy wagon with his older sister seated in it and tried to pull it as he walked backwards on the sidewalk. He grunted and heaved with all his might. I continued to hold the handle and let him lace his hands with mine. He became frustrated at first that I didn't let go, even trying to push me away. Gradually, he accepted my help and together we pulled the wagon down the sidewalk. Our progress was impeded by his tiny size and strength, and by his struggle to walk backwards without falling.

While watching my son Lawson trying to pull that wagon, I thought of the times in life where I've done the same thing. Stubbornly I try to take the reins, day after day. Stubbornly I have repeatedly forgotten and forsaken my "first love" (see Revelation 2:1-7) and have strayed from the path I should be walking. With my head bent down in concentration, I forged ahead.

And then, "I lift my eyes to the hills. From where does my help come? My help comes from the Lord, Who made Heaven and earth" (Psalm 121:1-2 ESV). I take my eyes off the pavement to see something much greater than I. My impatience to plow through my to-do list each day clouds my ability to see what is truly important.

When I have done that, I have been overconfident in my abilities and strength. Ever so gently He calls to me. I sense His presence as I tug and pull on a weight too heavy for me to move. He grips my hand and pulls along with me, but I know it's Him causing all the progress. He patiently allows me to pull by myself at times, knowing I will struggle and fall again. He never forces me to choose the right path, but reminds me constantly of my first love.

I sense that love in the peace that floods over me, even during times of great difficulty. His love is evident in His amazing creation. That love is visible when I behold the miracles of my children. That love is in His grace towards me and His willingness to take me back again and again. Even when I forget about Him, He never forgets about me. He loves me that much.

49. Accepting Help

During a shopping trip to Costco, my baby Evangeline was screaming in the checkout line. I was getting "the look" from other people in line. I took her out of her car seat and was trying to console her while pushing and pulling my two huge shopping carts and trying to pay. By this time, there were beads of sweat on my forehead and I was at my breaking point. I noticed a woman watching me from a distance. As soon as I finished paying, she and her husband came right over and he offered to help push my heavy, grocery-filled carts out to the car and load it all up for me. Normally I would have declined the offer, but the combination of the crying baby, my fatigue, and the windblown snow falling caused me to humble myself and say, "Yes, I'd love some help."

We humans can be such a stubborn, self-reliant bunch. It takes an awful lot to admit there's something with which I need help. That must be the reason I've been blessed with so many won-derful children who regularly bring me to my knees in defeat!

I can envision God watching us as our lives play out. He sees us as we wander through our days, asking in our moment of need, "Can I help you?" Often, we brush Him off: "I've got this, God. I'm good. Maybe another time." It's interesting how often the Bible refers to God as our Shepherd. He often has to lead, guide, and rescue us when we falter and fall down. I see the blessing in these moments where I'm brought low, because it brings me to a place where I am closer to God and can sense His presence more clearly, where my strength ends and His kicks in.

Where does my help come from? Where does your help come from?

50. It Goes Both Ways

"Don't hold the button down," my older son Carter screamed to his younger brother for the tenth time. They were playing (or trying to play) with the walkie-talkies again and it just wasn't working out. Lawson gets so excited the minute he realizes he can talk into the walkie-talkie that he grips it tightly and holds that button down, rambling on and on. It's a power trip for a little child I suppose. Carter never gets a chance to get a word in. He tries to be patient, but it's a one-sided conversation.

Listening to them play as the older one desperately tries to have a conversation with the younger, I saw a parallel to the way we often communicate with God. How many days are my prayers a long list of needs I lay out before Him? How often do I stop to listen and really be still so I can hear what He might say to me? The minute I realize I've got a captive audience, I'm quick to dominate the conversation. Then when things go awry, I'm just as quick to question God and wonder why my prayers aren't being answered the way I would like.

I've got to loosen my death-grip on that button. The key to answered prayer isn't getting in as many words as possible each day. The key is recognizing I have God's ear anytime, any place, and every day, and then humbly asking Him to help me through whatever life may throw my direction. He's waiting to talk to me if I'll just let go of the button and let Him speak.

51. The End and Scope of Life

"Wait for the Lord; be strong and take heart and wait for the Lord" (Psalm 27:14).

Life is filled to the brim with distractions. Everywhere we turn, there is something new vying for our time and attention. As I read Matthew not too long ago, a verse I had heard many times in the past spoke to me in a new way when I read it in the Amplified Version:

> She will bear a Son, and you shall call His name Jesus [the Greek form of the Hebrew Joshua, which means Savior], for He will save His people from their sins [*that is, prevent them from failing and missing the true end and scope of life, which is God*] (Matthew 1:21 AMPC, emphasis added).

What is the true end and scope of life? Do you often struggle with this as I do? Sometimes I need to get back to the basics, to step back from all the to-dos and distractions and just dwell on the essentials.

God tries in every way possible to lead me in the path I should take. "You're making a terrible mistake. I'm your parent and I know what is best for you. You may think this is good, but really it will only hurt you in the end. Don't lose sight of what's truly important. These things seem right and good to you for now, but they will never make you happy."

Can I let God be God? That is what it all comes down to. If I'm dead-set on making all the decisions, operating by my own playbook, then I leave little room for Him to dwell in and direct my life.

Heaven forbid I live out my years on this earth and miss the true end and purpose of it all! Repeatedly, and often in desperation sometimes, I kick my own pride to the curb and surrender my will to Him. The giants of *fear, discouragement, debilitating disease, grief, misunderstanding,* and *death* loom all around me and I say to God, "This is just too much for me. I need to do this my own way. You are asking too much of me." I passionately devote myself to things that serve as distractions from the pain. I self medicate on the temporary and ignore the eternal.

The truth is, I can't do it on my own. I'm too weak. I fall

on my face. I get to that point of utter desperation and that is where I cry out to God again, "Be God in my life!"

52. To God be the Glory

"Can't we go up the big hill. Can't we pleeeaaassseee go up the big hill?" asked my loquacious daughter who was pedaling on the tandem bicycle behind me. "Well, I guess we can try," I responded. She did have pedals that she'd occasionally push, but I was the one pulling her along for the entire ride. It was a humid 87 degrees and she wanted to go up the biggest hill in the neighborhood – a steep quarter-mile incline that gets my heart pounding even at a slow walk.

I looked up that hill, gritting my teeth and hoping I could propel the bike forward fast enough so that we didn't come to a stop and tip over. Up we went at a slow pace but finally we made it to the top. We made a turn and raced down the hill again, the wind refreshingly rushing by as we cruised down without having to pedal once. "Aren't you glad I came with you so I could help you pedal?" she asked me.

Oh, dear daughter, if you only knew! If you only realized that your meager pedaling efforts did virtually nothing to push us up the hill. If only you understood that having your bike attached to the back of mine did nothing but slow me down and made the ride so much more of an exertion for me.

As we began our initial ascent, I was thinking about how God carries me. I often think, in my limited human understanding, that I've got the wit, the know-how, and the strength to do things on my own. I have the audacity to think I can "help" God, when really I'm just tagging along for the ride, slowing Him down most of the time with my dead weight.

His mercies truly never cease to amaze me that He even gives me the opportunity to try, and has the patience to let me mess things up on a regular basis. We make it to the crest of one great obstacle and together coast down the other side. Quickly, just like that, I'm ready to take on the world again on my own, thinking I don't need Him or ignoring His presence and help.

May you not take for granted the help He offers you, day in and day out. Remember the way He carries you and your burdens and forgives your mistakes along the way. And when you reach that mountaintop, recognize that all the glory goes to Him: "For everything comes from him and exists by his power and is intended for his glory. All glory to him forever! Amen" (Romans 11:36 NLT).

Chapter 10

A Rainy Season

I've written a number of short stories about rain. Rain engages all our five senses. Rain often evokes an emotional response, whether it is joy for the life-sustaining moisture that keeps vegetation and wildlife alive or sorrow over plans that were impacted. It rained during my high school and college graduations, and on my wedding day, altering the original plans, so I know a thing or two about rain. But something the Lord has shown me is that rain is absolutely essential. Though rain may dampen our mood and plans, God can use it to grow us, strengthen us, and to elevate us to new levels of faith.

A rainy season is never easy to endure and we never know when it will end. Mine is stretching out far into the future with no immediate end in sight. The losses I have suffered and continue to suffer have transformed me. Having five young children to raise has presented its own set of challenges, but has also brought me great hope. Though I may not see a purpose in my rain, I wake up each day with a clear purpose to care for my kids and nurture and teach them things they'll need to know to make it in this world.

I can envision myself one day looking back on this time. The distinction between when my rainy season ended and a fruitful, more joyous season began will probably be blurred, perhaps even indistinguishable. How can that be, you may ask?

I believe in God's power to impart to us a joy that surpasses all understanding, a joy that can even be present in the rainy seasons of our lives. I believe this because I have personally experienced it again and again. On the days when I have needed Him the most and sought Him, I have always found Him, just as He promised me I would. He has given me the ability to smile, even in the midst of my tears of pain. While I could question His timing of experiencing so many losses in the mayhem of raising my young children, I realize it may have been the exact time I needed this the most.

My spirit is often buoyed by the things my children say to me, the things they do, and the lessons they teach me. I see myself in them so often, and my own relationship with God is reflected in the ways I treat Him like my children treat me. It has certainly been a humbling, powerful, and life-altering journey thus far.

Though I don't always understand the timing, I do need the rain when it comes. Without it, I would be weak. My faith would wither up and die. It brings me back to a place of need, a place where I truly wait on the Lord.

53. Freedom

The heavy downpour had come and gone in less than 10 minutes, but the ground was soaked and the air hung heavy with humidity. The kids started to venture back outside one by one and it was then that my husband noticed our dog, sniffing at something in the net covering our little strawberry patch. It was a beautiful red cardinal, tangled badly in the net and soaked from the rain. He was flapping frantically as he tried to escape. We quickly swung into action, my husband clipping carefully at the net with scissors while I tried to hold the bird in gloved hands. Little did I realize how sharp and powerful a cardinal's beak is. I could feel him chomping down on my fingers even through my husband's thick leather gloves. It was a little unnerving, but in minutes he was free again, no worse for wear, and he flew away to dry off.

I never like to see a creature suffer, and I find it ironic that when I'm trying to help one out, it fights me tooth and nail. How often do we do this very same thing with God? Regularly I am sure.

How often do we come upon difficult times and lash out

at God? How often do we blame Him for our tribulations, our sicknesses, or our pain?

How often is He waiting to help us, even offering us His comfort, mercy, compassion, and love, but we turn our backs on Him, curse Him, or spurn the One who has the power to help us?

That poor bird had no hope of survival if left alone. We were the only chance it had to make it out of that net, but when we stepped in to help, it wanted nothing more than to get me to release my hold so it could fly away.

Psalm 46:10 says, "Be still and know that I am God." When will we stop trying to free ourselves from all our predicaments and allow God to step in and handle them for us? When will we stop lashing out at the hand trying to save us? When will we stop turning our backs on God when things go wrong and start believing that He is *good* and well-intentioned, and that our single and greatest hope on this earth is His goodness?

I find incredible *freedom* when I let go of the circumstances that are outside my control and allow God to work in and through them. Note I never said that He shields me from difficulties; that isn't the way life works in a sin-tainted world. I have seen Him working in the midst of incredible trials in my own life. I will not and cannot imagine going through trials without having Him by my side. I keep my eyes fixed on the hope I have, in Him, and that hope gives me freedom from all the world can fling at me.

"Where the Spirit of the Lord is, there is freedom" (2 Corinthians 3:17).

54. Red, Yellow, Green

I peered out the window to see a beautiful and tranquil sunrise. The sky contained some swirling, wispy clouds that were picking up the gorgeous colors of the approaching sun: reds, oranges, pinks, purples and yellows. I attended to baby Evangeline, who was the reason I was even awake at such an early hour. After finishing with her, I left her room to see a huge flash of light fill the house. That was odd, for just 20 minutes ago the sky was clear.

Sure enough, as I looked out, there were ominous black clouds filling the sky and signaling that a storm was near.

During the summer months, I occasionally take the kids swimming and one of the pools we visit requires the kids to wear a necklace. Those who are strong swimmers and pass a swim test get a green necklace. Those who can swim a little but aren't strong swimmers get a yellow necklace. Those who can't swim at all must wear a red necklace.

My oldest, Carter, wanted to take the swim test so he could go down the waterslide. He sliced through the water with ease, treaded water, and hopped out of the pool, excited to be decorated with his "trophy," the green necklace. My daughter Reese, bolstered by his success, wanted to give it a try next. Halfway down the length of the pool, it was obvious she wasn't going to make it. As the water grew deeper and deeper, her eyes widened with panic. Her strokes grew weaker and she grabbed onto the ledge for safety. The lifeguard turned to me and said, "I don't think she's a strong enough swimmer yet." I agreed.

As we left the indoor pool and went back outside, my younger son Lawson brazenly took off for the deep end of the pool before I could even put his life jacket on. His red necklace was clearly visible, proclaiming to everyone, "I can't swim!" Later I thought of the verses in Isaiah 42:2-3:

> "When you go through deep waters, I will be with you. When you go through rivers of difficulty, you will not drown. When you walk through the fire of oppression, you will not be burned up; the flames will not consume you" (NLT).

Are you ready for a storm? Are you ready for the deep water? Sometimes there is no warning; we are coasting along with little awareness of what is about to hit and when it does, we are tested and challenged to the depths of our strength and character. When that storm hits, and it certainly will, will you have the strength and courage to wade or swim through those churning waters to safety, or will you flounder? Will you allow fear to paralyze you? Or will you foolishly plunge into waters far too deep for you to survive? A storm is approaching. How will you prepare?

Will you fall back on your own abilities when the wind is raging and sky is opening up? Will you have the strength on your own? I know I won't, for my strength, my peace in the storm, and my hope all come from the Lord.

> Then they cried to the Lord in their trouble, and He brought them out of their distresses. He caused the storm to be still, so that the waves of the sea were hushed. Then they were glad because they were quiet, so He guided them to their desired haven (Psalm 107:28-30 NASB).

55. Facing the Storm

> "So do not fear, for I am with you; do not be dismayed, for I am your God. I will strengthen you and help you; I will uphold you with my righteous right hand" (Isaiah 41:10).

A loud clap of thunder seemed to shake the whole car as the kids and I quickly piled in. I was getting them all buckled into their seats when a huge flash appeared with almost instantaneous thunder, so loud it made everyone jump. "That was really close," proclaimed Carter. Lawson was trembling and crying. He was terrified, whimpering for most of the ride home.

We drove through pouring rain, so hard I could barely see. As I drove through enormous puddles, they splashed up on both sides of the van and onto the windshield, adding to my lack of visibility. The rain then turned to hail but then almost as quickly as it had started, the storm passed. A few miles down the road, the clouds gave way to blue sky. Within ten minutes, we drove from a deluge with frightening lightning, thunder, and hail, to sunshine and dry roads.

I was planting some seedlings in the garden that same night and more dark clouds were looming on the horizon. My husband, who was working beside me, said casually, "Looks like it's going to rain again," and with that my son went into hysterics all over again.

My daughter Sienna sat near me and we chatted as I planted, still keeping an eye on the sky. "Isn't it amazing," I asked her, "how little droplets of water can float up into the sky and form clouds that can make such powerful storms with thunder and lightning and rain and hail?"

"How do little water drops do all that?" she asked me with wonder in her eyes.

"God sure was creative when He created all of these things, wasn't He?"

"Yes," she answered.

I find myself navigating through some terrifying storms these days, trying to break free of the deluge of trouble or make sense of it all in the day-to-day. I know the clouds have to break, that there is still hope on the horizon, but oh how those storms batter and terrify me at times. The words of Isaiah encourage me as I face these mighty tempests. I can envision myself walking into the storm, and there is a large hand pressing up behind me. It's the loving hand of God, holding me upright while also pushing me forward. There is no turning back. I must press on and continue to fight the good fight. I will not fear.

56. The Need for Rain

I pushed the baby in her little swing as I kept my eyes on the horizon. Dark clouds were looming, indicating that another summer storm was fast-approaching. I heard a distant rumble of thunder and ushered the kids indoors to safety. The sky was transformed from bright sunshine to ominous cloud cover. Then the rains came, first in big droplets and then in wind-driven sheets. The parched earth seeming to breathe a sigh of relief and thanksgiving for the much-needed moisture. After a time, the clouds departed, the summer heat crept back in, and the storm was over.

As each new day dawns, in my first waking moments I am faced with a choice. My burdens and heartaches are waiting to meet me again, ready to take my joy, fill up my time, and steal my resolve. I must make a decision.

I was made for much more than just being a feeble creature, carried along by the whim of my emotions. I was made to be strong, persevere, and even flourish through the tests and storms of life. Dark clouds are always visible in the distance, waiting to rush in if I allow them the opportunity. I must hold fast to Him and gaze steadily into His unfathomable, brilliant light.

As the day came to a close, I happened to look out and saw a glorious pink and purple sunset. I stepped outside just to take it in for a few moments. The sunset cast an eerie pink glow on everything; it was truly magnificent. There were many dead leaves on the ground under one particular tree in our yard. My daughter Reese followed me out and asked, "What happened to the tree?" Intense summer heat with no rain during the previous week had caused some of the leaves to die and fall off. The wind from the storm had knocked all the leaves to the ground, scattering them all over the grass.

We likewise experience these seasons of drought and the storms of life. We long for sunny skies and gentle showers, but this is not always our reality. Sometimes the storm hits us with a force that knocks away some of our resolve, shakes us to the core, and brings us to our knees. When I find myself knees down to the ground, I realize that this is the perfect posture for prayer. I turn to the One who brings me meaning and the strength to go on. I look to Him for my hope and for peace in the midst of the storm. I need the rain. It is a necessity and it reminds me of my deep, desperate, and daily need for Him and His protection.

SECTION THREE

NEW EVERY MORNING

You will surely forget your trouble,
recalling it only as waters gone by.
Life will be brighter than noonday,
and darkness will become like morning.
You will be secure, because there is hope;
you will look about you and take your rest in safety.

Job 11:16–18

Chapter 11
Life in the Midst

I sat on the hammock swing with my mom the other day, gazing out over the rolling hills as we chatted. The beauty did not escape me. We only need to open our eyes to see it surrounding us. Fall leaves lit up the landscape with splashes of red, orange, and yellow. An autumn breeze blew gently over us as we rocked back and forth. As frantic and overscheduled as life can be, there are times, sacred times, when I get the rare opportunity to slow down and just be present. It may be for just a few minutes but these times are precious.

I savor these moments and try to store them away in my memory. I will not have so many more like this with just my mom and me. I'm losing her, piece by piece, to an insidious and incurable illness. Many of my hopes and dreams for this stage of my life are dying as well, with my mom finally living close to me after being separated by 400 miles for 17 years. Now she is close by geographically, but slips farther away from me day by day.

Life is so intense and overwhelming at times. Sometimes the very act of dragging my weary body out of bed in the morning seems too much. Alongside my amazing husband, I'm trying to raise five young children and be as supportive and helpful to my mom as I can be, all while still grieving the loss of my brother. It is during my moments of helplessness that the Lord intervenes with an infusion of His strength and inspiration. Right smack in the midst of these troubling times, God has given me hope. Time after time, He has filled me with insight and strength through the simplest things – things I read or listen to on the radio, or things my kids say and do. If God is an artist, my life is His canvas. If God is my teacher, the simple day-to-day chaos of parenting five kids has been my classroom. I share these simple stories and lessons He is teaching me, so that perhaps you too might experience Him "in the midst."

God has spoken and I have taken note. He has awakened me to many truths of which previously I had no sense or concept. He has drawn me away from my self-centered way of living and shown me something much better.

Life in the midst is messy. I feel a lot like someone who is learning to sail a boat. My path is seldom a straight line but rather a jagged zigzag of trying and trying again to get it right. When will it get easier? It does get easier, right? I cry out to the Lord, and He answers me. I draw near to Him and He draws near to me: "Draw near to God and He will draw near to you" (James 4:8 NKJV).

Life does feel a lot like a ship sailing on stormy seas. Sometimes we bob along, just waiting for the next big storm to hit. When those storms hit, do we try to navigate through them alone? I've found a better way.

> But to as many as did receive and welcome Him, He gave the authority (power, privilege, right) to become the children of God, that is, to those who believe in (adhere to, trust in, and rely on) His name (John 1:12 AMPC).

Suddenly, life doesn't seem so uncertain anymore. Situations seem more manageable. We see what Christ did for us, the ways He suffered for us, all He offers us, and it gives us hope. I believe in, adhere to, trust in, and rely on His name. If I only had my strength to rely on, I would not have a leg to stand on. He offers me life in the midst of darkness and death. It has taken me far too many years and a season of reaching my rock bottom to realize that He is my all, to recognize that the joy of the Lord can be experienced even in our darkest hours.

This is what I long to share with you. This is the message I want to convey in the final section of this book. Even as I write these words, I am still suffering, but sharing God's hope with those around me gives me strength, purpose, and the will to carry on.

57. Perspective – A View from on High

I was standing at the kitchen sink washing the dirty breakfast dishes. Pausing to look out the window for a minute, I happened to see a small airplane jetting across the pastel morning sky.

Do you remember the first time you flew in an airplane? The first time I was really aware of it was an amazing experience. Up until then, my view of the world was so flat! I had never experienced anything like the perspective I gained when I was 30,000 feet up in the sky looking down on the world. To me, nothing can better enlighten a person as to the vastness of the planet we live on. (Okay, maybe space travel, but that's not in the cards for me anytime soon.)

When you are down here on the ground, it's easy to get wrapped up in the day-to-day grind. It's all too natural to get distracted or consumed by everything that's going on around you. From time to time, it's a good practice to get out of that linear kind of living and put things in perspective from on-high. Much of what we fret and fritter away our days thinking about is quite insignificant.

When we are on top of a mountain or up in an airplane, we can see so much farther than when we are standing on the ground at sea level. Our whole perspective changes. God has this same kind of "far-out, future vision" for our lives. He can see the future way beyond our short lives. His perspective is much higher, wider, deeper, and more real than anything we will ever experience. It's easy to get wrapped up in what's happening today, and then frustrated when He doesn't answer our prayers in the way we think best. We are looking at life from sea-level view and He is looking down from on high.

When I stop to consider the vast universe we live in and how very small I am compared to the planet we live on, the solar system we spin through, the galaxy we occupy, and the expanse of space much greater than the human mind can grasp, it causes me to pause and put things in perspective. It causes me to be grateful for this chance to live and love, to teach and be taught. It helps me remember there is often more at stake than what meets my eye. It's all a matter of perspective. Even the most difficult time in life or most difficult obstacle can seem like a mere blip on the radar when I put it in the context of an entire lifetime. When things seem to be spinning out of control and I need a reality check, I pray God will give me a glimpse of the situation from on high.

> But because of his great love for us, God, who is rich in mercy, made us alive with Christ even when we were dead in transgressions—it is by grace you have been saved. And God raised us up with Christ and seated us with him in the heavenly realms in Christ Jesus, in order that in the coming ages he might show the incomparable riches of his grace, expressed in his kindness to us in Christ Jesus. For it is by grace you have been saved, through faith—and this is not from yourselves, it is the gift of God—not by works, so that no one can boast. For we are God's handiwork, created in Christ Jesus to do good works, which God prepared in advance for us to do (Ephesians 2:4-10).

58. Metamorphosis

You've probably heard the saying, "change is good." Who really embraces change when it comes, however, without a little hesitancy? Change can be difficult. It is also life-altering and most times unavoidable. The truth is, most people don't like it.

I remember learning about forest fires in school as a young child. I grew up near the Pine Barrens in New Jersey. As I watched a video about forest fires, there was this odd phenomenon that caught my attention. Certain pine cones would only open up and release their seeds during the heat of a forest fire. It would seem that the fire would be a bad thing, but it burns up a lot of old dead trees, weeds, and other junk that aren't good for the forest. Then those special pine cones would release their seeds to start a whole new forest. What could be perceived as a negative situation in actuality was a positive one in the interests of the forest's health.

Fast forwarding to my life now, there is a simple illustration I've been able to share with my children, all because of the fennel my husband plants in our backyard garden each year. Fennel attracts Swallowtail caterpillars to the garden. They are beautiful when we get a close look at them. The first time we found them, I explained to the kids a little about how the caterpillar changes into a butterfly. "Does the caterpillar die?" the kids asked. Well, in a way I guess it does, but what it turns into is so much more beautiful.

Metamorphosis profoundly alters one's appearance, inner character, or situation. The Lord can bring beauty from ashes. He can take even the most awful situation and bring good from it. I am clinging to that hope; I am trusting in His plan for me and for my family.

> The Spirit of the Sovereign Lord is on me, because the Lord has anointed me to proclaim good news to the poor. He has sent me to bind up the brokenhearted, to proclaim freedom for the captives and release from darkness for the prisoners, to proclaim the year of the Lord's favor and the day of vengeance of our God, to comfort all who mourn, and provide for those who grieve in Zion—to bestow on them a crown of beauty instead of ashes, the oil of joy instead of mourning, and a garment of praise instead of a spirit of despair. They will be called oaks of righteousness, a planting of the Lord for the display of his splendor (Isaiah 61:1-3).

59. Two Big Bottles of Joy

The old saying "the best things in life are free" is so true. My husband walked in the door one day, returning from a Costco run, with two huge jugs of soap and plopped them down on the counter top. "Look Mama," my daughter said excitedly, "we got you soap for your birthday!" I had to laugh at that! I use Joy soap for making homemade bubbles for the kids.

Two big bottles of Joy just for me. If only joy could be obtained that easily! Finding real and lasting joy is much more complicated. My mantra lately seems to be this: *My joy is not determined by my circumstances.* If joy isn't determined by circumstances, where can we find it? Well, it certainly can't be bought. My kids can help me experience joy for a time, but then when their behavior tanks, I'm left feeling a void again.

I stopped yesterday to look closely at a butterfly. I admired the colors and beautiful patterns on its wings, the delicacy and perfection of this amazing creature. Then I admired the vibrant colors of my newly-planted flowers. It had not been an easy week in many ways. I was struggling to overcome both physical and emotional pains that weighed me down and tried to drag me under. In the midst of even this, however, there are glimpses of beauty and joy.

Sitting in church one Sunday, I fixed my eyes on a verse displayed on a banner at the front of the sanctuary, "Be joyful in hope, patient in affliction, faithful in prayer" (Romans 12:12).

That's the answer, really, if I'm looking for a formula for joy. I am not filled with joy from the things of this world but as a result of my hope in God. I must be patient to trust in His timing, even when I am afflicted by many trials. What's more, I must be faithful to be in constant prayer, even on the craziest, most trying days, knowing ultimately that He cares for me.

60. Overflowing

"Why did God make puff balls?"

I dug up a bucketful of dandelions from the yard, which really seemed like a wasted effort in the end when I looked out and still saw hundreds of them speckling our lawn. My oldest daughter Reese helped me for a little while and we talked about how beautiful a puff ball is, even though it is a weed. "Well, why did He make puff balls?" she wanted to know.

"You know, I'm really not sure." I told her about my childhood wonder when I encountered a puff ball and how I always wanted to blow those wispy white seeds away when I found one, much to my poor dad's dismay. It seemed we fought a losing battle with the dandelions in our yard year after year.

Life isn't always smooth sailing. It is often pock-marked by difficulties, trials, and sadness, similar to the sea of dandelions that overtake my yard every spring. Maybe there is something to be learned from the lowly dandelion. For as many as I dug up, I'd guess that three-fourths of them were literally growing on a rock. I could feel the rock as I dug underground to break off the roots. In a place so hard where nothing else could grow, that is where the dandelion took root. You've got to give them some props for that!

You may be in a rock hard place right now, a place where it feels like nothing can grow and any hope of good is futile. What kind of root system do you have? Will you survive?

When our roots are in Him, they go deep. When it feels like we are in a place where no life can flourish, we will find the true meaning, importance, and vitality that comes from faith. The idea that faith can lead to gratitude – overflowing thankfulness – is certainly counterintuitive and counter-cultural. The world would have us think that we deserve to whine when life isn't fair, that we are justified in our rants and self-sponsored pity parties when things aren't going our way.

The next time you hit a rock, how will you react? Thankfulness isn't an innate human characteristic – at least not for me. When I stop to dwell upon the Lord and bask in the understanding of His love for me, I start to realize that the circumstances I'm going through today should never be allowed to distract me from the many ways He has blessed and continues to bless me.

61. Anxious Thoughts and Heavenly Peace

His little brow was deeply furrowed with concern as his

sister screamed out in distress. He came over and compassionately gave her the biggest hug his little arms could give, patting her back with one hand. "It's okay," he told her. I love watching a toddler offer comfort to his older sibling. She was hurting and he offered calm and reassuring comfort. Isn't that a perfect reminder of what God does for us?

Philippians 4:6-7 says, "Do not be anxious about anything, but in every situation, by prayer and petition, with thanksgiving, present your requests to God. And the peace of God, which transcends all understanding, will guard your hearts and your minds in Christ Jesus."

Anxious thoughts prevent us from experiencing the true joy that we were meant to have. They trap us in a downward spiral of worry, fear, and doubt, blinding us to anything happening around us that is good. Anxious thoughts shift away our focus from what is truly important. Worry can overtake us in the blink of an eye, even on our best days, and there are so many things we can worry about: finances, relationships, safety, health, even our own value and self-worth.

God offers us comfort in the midst of this worry, however, for He *promises* to be there for us and alongside us in the day-to-day grind. He lets us know it is going to be okay. His sweet embrace came to us in the form of a helpless baby, reminding us what heavenly peace truly looks like.

When my head hits the pillow at night, do I have many thoughts still racing around or do I have peace? The blissful sleep of a young child is precious to observe. No matter the events of the day, they are not tormented. They depend on someone else for everything so therefore have no concept of fear or worry. They have total trust in their caretaker, and that trust should be what we strive for also. "Can any one of you by worrying add a single hour to his life?" (Matthew 6:27).

Where do you put your hope and trust? When you truly put your trust in God, you need not worry or fear. Cast all of your cares on Him, and just wait to see what happens. Why waste another minute in worry? Give your burdens over to the One who cares for even the tiniest sparrow. Accept the gift of peace that He offers you in the midst of this crazy life. When you do, you will increasingly sense the indescribable blessing of His heavenly peace.

62. His Marvelous Light

But you are a chosen people, a royal priesthood,
a holy nation, a people for God's own possession,
to proclaim the virtues of Him who called you
out of darkness into His marvelous light (1 Peter 2:9).

We are creatures designed to live in the light. I crave it, looking forward to the sunrise every day. Light has an instant medicinal quality for me, and gives me a boost for my emotional state, stamina, and appreciation for each day. The light heals the pains of the dark night and brings renewal and refreshment. I love the months of summer with the longer days, which give me extra time to spend in natural sunlight.

The verse included above from 1 Peter caused me to think about how God has called us out of darkness and into His marvelous light. He illuminates my soul with His truths, He brings light to my darkest days and offers hope in the situations that seem to lack any.

When I stop to dwell on the truly difficult situations in my life, I have an image of God coming near me while I am in that overwhelming pain. As He draws near, the scene around me begins to fade away as His light becomes brighter and brighter until all I can see is Him.

As I study the lives of great men and women of the faith, I am touched by how many of them suffered, far beyond what I have ever experienced, yet they were still able to praise God in the midst of their sufferings. How were they able to accomplish such a feat? It goes back to this same idea of the light. They were called into His light, and when the things of this world faded into the background, they were able to focus solely on the One who gives us light. John 8:12 says, "I am the Light of the world. Whoever follows Me will never walk in darkness but will have the light of life."

How can I survive this unrelenting pain? How can I wake up day after day and not lose all hope? It is all a matter of focus. Do I focus on me or on God? Do I dwell on the temporal or the eternal? Do I question the "fairness" of a life of which I understand so little or trust in His plan for me? My hands are so tightly clinging to what I think is my "stake" or my "choice" in my life.

Slowly, ever so slowly, my grip loosens. I relinquish my control and surrender it to God. I am broken as I cry out to Him and ask Him to take whatever is left of me and use it for His purposes and glory. His light floods my heart in a way I can't deny or ignore and in that moment of surrender, I praise Him because He is right by my side. This is truly life in the midst. I cannot ignore His love for it is with me always – and has been there all along.

Chapter 12
Love Letters

"How can you believe in a God who allows such terrible things to happen in the world?" This is a question I've been asked a few times and one I have pondered myself. How can God sit back and watch over this mess and not intervene? Why doesn't He answer my prayers for rescue? If He is truly all powerful, why doesn't He right all the wrongs or prevent them from happening in the first place? And my troubles are only the tip of the iceberg when I stop to see what is happening the world over.

My human inclination in these times is to react according to my emotions, to the pain I am feeling, and pull away. "He must not care. He must not honor His promises. How can I praise Him when this world is crashing down around me?"

When we read through Genesis, we barely make it through the stunning story of creation before the plot takes a twist. A cunning serpent enters the scene and catches Eve off guard: "Did God really say, 'You must not eat from any tree in the garden'?" (Genesis 3:1). The serpent spoke lies back then and he is speaking them to our hearts even now. He urges us to question whether God has our best interests in mind or not. We wonder if He is withholding something better from us and we question His intentions for us. Eating the forbidden fruit gave us the ability to judge between right and wrong, good and evil, when we should always defer to Him for that understanding.

Do you sense the love of God in your life, even in the hard times? I have and it has shocked me, for I found God where and when I least expected Him. I also didn't anticipate that my faith would grow during trials or that I would feel a greater depth of His love during such a painful season. Our God is thankfully not bound by our meager human perceptions of Him!

I was sorting through a large stack of papers on my desk the other day and came across many letters I had saved – letters from friends, family, or that my kids had written to me. These are my treasures and I cannot throw them away. The kids had written things like "You are the best Mom ever!" and "You are osum!" (which is awesome in five-year-old spelling). There were letters from friends sharing how God has been working in their lives, even despite their own set of difficulties. These are words of sustenance, encouragement, and most importantly, love.

God too sends me frequent "letters." My days are a series of love letters penned in the most breathtaking sunrises, gentle breezes, dewdrops on a spider's delicate web, the fragrance of a rose, the piercing blue sky, a surreal rainbow, and a full moon rising up from the horizon on a crystal clear night. God answers my prayers in His way, in His time, and in perfect harmony with His will for my life. I have seen it happen again and again and every time, it takes my breath away. Something will happen that stops me in my tracks as I realize that He has been at work in my life when I didn't even know it. Not too long ago, I witnessed six rainbows in only one week. Was that just a coincidence? Each time one arrived, it was a time I needed that extra boost and reminder that He loves me.

There are love letters from God at every turn. Sometimes I need to get over myself and my expectations, and ask Him to help me see the truth of His love for me.

63. His Eye is on the Sparrow

I vividly remember a Sunday morning at church many years ago, when a young boy sang *His Eye is on the Sparrow*. He stood all alone as he sang with no music accompanying him. It was a beautiful song, with a beautiful message, sung by one so young and innocent. That is one memory I will have for a lifetime. I've never heard another rendition that comes even close to his.

I ran across what Jesus said in Luke 12:6-7 and it gave me pause to think: "Are not five sparrows sold for two pennies? Yet not one of them is forgotten by God. Indeed, the very hairs of your head are all numbered. Don't be afraid; you are worth more than many sparrows." Then I saw a similar verse in Matthew 10:29, which says, "Are not two sparrows sold for a penny? Yet not one of them will fall to the ground outside your Father's care."

How great is God's care for us! As a frail being, I am tempted to worry about every little thing. Why do I fritter away so much of my time in worry after I read passages like these? Not even the sparrows, so common we hardly even take notice of them, are forgotten by God.

Worry is my way of playing God, of trying to hold onto the reins of my life. How much does my worry detract from my focus on God and His provision for me? Do I let it get to the point where it actually draws me away from God? When I see a sparrow now, I will always remember these verses and how much He cares for me, watching over me all the time.

64. Pursuit

I'm standing in a dark living room, eyes closed and a slight smile on my face as I finish slowly counting to 20. I can hear little feet still scrambling, muffled laughter, furniture being moved, and loud whispers. We are playing a game of hide-and-seek where I am the perpetual seeker and my kids are ever trying to find the perfect hiding spot. They never tire of this game and their favorite part is when I come looking for them. As little children, we are thrilled by games of pursuit. We love to hide but we really want to be found.

When I shout, "Ready or not, here I come," they giggle with delight, usually revealing their not-good-to-begin-with hiding spots. My daughter Sienna will often cry out, "I'm in the closet," or "I'm under the table" before I even have a chance to start looking. She is excited for me to find her and can't wait to tell me how I can get to her as quickly as possible. They are even more delighted when I sneak up and find them with no help from them, often feigning surprise at their "amazing" hiding places. There is never a fear in their minds that I will abandon the game and leave them hiding forever. They have complete and total trust that I, their loving parent, will keep on looking for them until I find them.

Our innocence fades all too quickly and we are no longer interested in childhood games. The hiding places aren't big enough to fit our adult frames anyway. We move on to other games of hide-and-seek. We go looking for all kinds of things, some of them worthy of our efforts, others not so much. Some people are desperately pursuing someone or hoping that someone will pursue them. We also pursue things like sports, hobbies, cooking, career advancement, adventure, money, popularity, power, beauty, knowledge, and the list goes on and on. When those pursuits become an obsession, then we are engaged in what the Bible calls idolatry, and we can take the simplest thing and make it an idol.

If only we could hang on to some of that childhood innocence and trust. I wish I had more of it when it came to my faith in the One who is constantly pursuing me. A short passage in Isaiah gripped my heart recently:

> "Can a mother forget the baby at her breast and have no compassion on the child she has borne? Though she may forget, I will not forget you! See, I have engraved you on the palms of my hands" (Isaiah 49:15-16).

Now there's a promise I can hang onto and appreciate on my most difficult days. He hasn't forgotten about me, though I may try to hide from Him in my day-to-day routine of watching the children and doing household chores, cooking and cleaning, and all the other "important" things. I hide myself in my never-ending to-do list, thinking I'm well-hidden from Him. Yet He is always there pursuing me. I may even call out when things get really hectic, "God, I'm still here, have you forgotten about me?"

And of course I know He hasn't.

65. The Mercy Seat

Praised (honored, blessed) be the God and Father
of our Lord Jesus Christ (the Messiah)! By His
boundless mercy we have been born again to
an ever-living hope through the resurrection of
Jesus Christ from the dead, [Born anew] into an
inheritance which is beyond the reach of change
and decay [imperishable], unsullied and unfading,
reserved in heaven for you, Who are being
guarded (garrisoned) by God's power through
[your] faith [till you fully inherit that final]
salvation that is ready to be revealed [for you] in
the last time (1 Peter 1:3-5 AMPC).

As we wrapped up a long and challenging day during
which three of my kids had made some poor choices, just one
word echoed in my mind: *mercy*. Mercy is an amazing concept,
and God's mercy is not just any mercy, but mercy we can count
on – free and undeserved: "But I have trusted, leaned on, and been
confident in Your mercy and loving-kindness; my heart shall rejoice and be in high spirits in Your salvation" (Psalm 13:5 AMPC).

I am told to show mercy because God has graciously extended it to me. My children must be guided and disciplined, but
also must sense what it means to experience mercy. I am confident
of God's mercy for me. It started when I was born again. Time and
again I fail Him when I sin.

How can I more fully reflect this kind of mercy to the
people I encounter every day? May I ever dwell on and be reminded of what God has done for me and share it with everyone
I meet.

*Lord, let it be that I, my actions, my words and my heart, might
be a reflection of Your boundless mercy.*

66. True Love

"I mow the lawn tonight. You help me." My determined son Lawson said this to me as he grabbed his little plastic Fisher-Price lawnmower out of the shed, then went back in to push the real lawnmower out for me. "Okay, I'll help you." As I mowed, he followed right along behind me with his own little mower, keeping up for at least the first 20 minutes. Eventually he tired out and disappeared into the backyard.

I had to chuckle at his adorable insistence that he, a two-year-old at the time, was so sure he was going to mow the entire lawn with his little toy mower. Sure he went through the motions of mowing and made a valiant effort in the beginning, but it was too great a task for him to do on his own. His mower wasn't the right tool for the job and he didn't have the strength or an understanding of how to complete the job.

That night as I was putting my sleepy son to bed, I saw an enormous rainbow arcing through the dark sky. "Look," I said, "a big rainbow!"

He climbed out of bed to look out the window with me for a few moments, in awe of the amazing sight. "What's that, Mama?"

"That is a rainbow," I responded. "Do you know what it means? It means that God loves us."

I tucked him in and gave him a big kiss, thankful to have shared this moment of beauty and profound truth with him. How often have I gone to the Lord and said, "Lord, let's do this together." I have all the right intentions, even recognizing my need for His strength and wisdom, but then, just like my son, I stubbornly try to take charge. All too soon, I fall short and recognize my need for Him even more. In spite of the fact that I repeat this scenario again and again, He still loves me.

67. Water and Sunshine

It was another windy morning as I sat on my bed, looking out the window as I prayed. The breeze shook the trees and blew the leaves every which way. The sound was powerful, like a mighty, rushing wind that was referred to in the Bible.

We spent a morning one time visiting friends who have a lake in their backyard. The kids loved exploring this magical mini-ecosystem. Fish ate bread from their hands, along with some curious baby mallards. A big, green frog provided a great show as he swam away from his gleeful onlookers using his powerful legs to do so.

The fingerprints of the Lord are everywhere I look in creation. Though we may not physically see Him, just like that early morning wind, He is undeniably there. He makes His presence known through the complexity, the order, the dramatic beauty and creativity we see, if only we would take the time to look.

It's these moments that are easily overlooked, the leaves blowing in the breeze or a peaceful morning by a pond, that speak to me most clearly. God gives me these opportunities to see Him, to recognize His involvement in these everyday events. He beckons for me to step away from the din of life and fellowship with Him. I love a passage in 1 Kings 19 where Elijah is waiting to encounter God. There is an earthquake and then a fire, but God was not in either of those. Then he heard a gentle blowing, a mere whisper, and that was where he met God:

> But the Lord said to him, "What are you doing here, Elijah?"
>
> Elijah replied, "I have zealously served the Lord God Almighty. But the people of Israel have broken their covenant with you, torn down your altars, and killed every one of your prophets. I am the only one left, and now they are trying to kill me, too."
>
> "Go out and stand before me on the mountain," the Lord told him. And as Elijah stood there, the Lord passed by, and a mighty windstorm hit the mountain. It was such a terrible blast that the rocks were torn loose, but the Lord was not in the wind. After the wind there was an earthquake, but the Lord was not in the

earthquake. And after the earthquake there was a fire, but the Lord was not in the fire. And after the fire there was the sound of a gentle whisper. When Elijah heard it, he wrapped his face in his cloak and went out and stood at the entrance of the cave (1 Kings 19:9–13 NLT).

Don't ignore those whispers or the miraculous revealed in the mundane. There are moments every single day when I am awed by some aspect of creation, an awe that reminds me to give credit to the Creator and appreciate all that He has done for me. I serve a God who delights in the details and He does all this not for Himself, but for me!

68. Pockets

Little feet come to a stop in my open doorway as early morning light filters around the short silhouette. I lift my head to see what time it is and who is awake already. There stands my son Lawson with both hands plunged deep into his pockets. Oh how he loves those pockets! Not too long ago, he didn't know pockets existed, but now he will not wear a pair of pants without them.

Pockets are where he stores his most prized possessions, things like a set of play keys, an acorn, a coin found on the sidewalk, a piece of candy, or a few stickers. Pockets have opened up a whole new world to him, giving him a place to store things that are special and valuable to him. One night after his bath, I dared to put some pajama pants on him. This was met with angry protests as he ran from the bathroom to ditch his pajamas in favor of some shorts with pockets.

We come into this world without a single possession to our name. We grow older and begin to learn quickly the concept of "mine." How similar I am to my little son, cherishing the things of this world, digging deep into my pockets to touch the things I love, making sure they are still there, still mine. How hard it is to give up my treasures, to open my fists and let go of the past, all the things I've been storing deep in the pockets of my heart for so many years. How hesitant I am to offer up my objects of comfort, the bits and pieces I've collected over the last few decades that meant so much to me. Oh, the folly of investing so much of my time and attention in things that are temporal and meaningless in the grand scheme of life.

If only I could clearly see past the here-and-now and obtain a clearer concept of my future destiny that would inspire me to store my treasure for the future. *I miss out on so much by hanging on to so much.* I waste time, lose energy, cause pain, misplace priorities, and miss opportunities by focusing on my earthly treasures.

God, turn my pockets inside-out! Give me a glimpse of Your glory, and the riches that await me in Heaven someday. Help me to see You, know You, and trust You and your plan for me. Help me to eagerly anticipate all that awaits me in Heaven and to take hold of the life in You that is truly life.

> Command those who are rich in this present world not to be arrogant nor to put their hope in wealth, which is so uncertain, but to put their hope in God, who richly provides us with everything for our enjoyment. Command them to do good, to be rich in good deeds, and to be generous and willing to share. In this way they will lay up treasure for themselves as a firm foundation for the coming age, so that they may take hold of the life that is truly life (1 Timothy 6:17-19).

69. A Safe Place

I walked slowly up the hillside in the backyard, watching our bluebird box carefully as I approached it. Four gorgeous blue eggs appeared in the box a few days earlier, much to the kids' delight. Our resident bluebirds have returned for another nesting season, gracing our yard with their flowery songs and flashes of brilliant blue feathers.

As I neared the box, my eyes scanned the nearby trees. Sure enough, just 20 feet away, the mother bluebird sat in a tree, ever watchful of her precious eggs. I knew she would be nearby.

It made me think of a verse: "He will cover you with his feathers, and under his wings you will find refuge; his faithfulness will be your shield and rampart" (Psalm 91:4).

When my youngest daughter Evangeline was a newborn, her favorite place to nap was while she was in my arms, or riding in her backpack on my chest. And why wouldn't it be her resting place of choice? She knew I was right there with her because she could feel, smell, and hear me. She knew she was in a safe place and it brought her total peace.

What could be more beautiful than the love and devotion of a parent for their child? It is a distinct reminder of God's love for me. Though I face many days when it is tempting to blame God for my problems or to ignore Him like a defiant teenager, the abundance of His grace washes away my wrong thinking and constantly brings me back to the remembrance of His love for me.

He loves me with the fierce protectiveness that parents have for their children. He sees me in all my frailty and helplessness and desires the best for me. Even on my worst days, He would still have died for me. As I gaze lovingly into the face of my sweet baby, I'm all too aware that my imperfect human love is but a shallow and weak comparison to the depths of His love for me, for her, and for all of humanity.

Aren't we all longing for a safe place to rest our weary heads? Closeness brings comfort. While the storms of life may rage furiously around me, I am at peace, knowing He is near, and He loves me without measure.

Chapter 13
Run and not Grow Weary

One of my favorite passages that I memorized as a teenager is found in Isaiah 40:29-31:

> He gives strength to the weary and increases the power of the weak. Even youths grow tired and weary, and young men stumble and fall; but those who hope in the Lord will renew their strength. They will soar on wings like eagles; they will run and not grow weary, they will walk and not be faint.

A hope renewed. That is the promise to me, the extraordinary power of hope that appears out of nowhere, at times when I least expect it. When I'm so weary that I can barely walk, then the flood of His strength comes rushing in. When I've reached the end of my rope, He will not leave me hanging. I hope in Him, not because I expect Him to answer my prayers in the way I want Him to, but rather because of the future He has promised me. And He has never broken a promise. I hope because of what He has done for me already, sending His Son to die for me, forgiving me, and offering me many second chances.

Faith untested is not really faith at all. If that's true, then I have true faith because I have been pushed to the edge. I have come to a place in my life where I lay down my own pursuits and ask Him to hand me a cross and take it up. In an odd way, when I lay down my own priorities and will, I find the hope to press on. I have renewed strength because I am not pursuing the things of this world. I behold His greatness and it offers such promise. Now I can soar with the eagles like the promise in Isaiah, rather than stumble along, lost in my own attempts to run without Him.

70. Pacing

I took my son Carter with me on a run one morning. He was eager to run in a 5K race with me sometime, or a fun race where the runners dash through colored bubbles, get sprayed with colored powder, or work their way through challenging obstacles. He had never run in a race before and had never really run longer than a mile, so I warned him that he needed to start training. As we began our run, I told him that the most important thing he needed to remember if he wants to run a longer distance is to pace himself. If he went out too fast, he would never make it to the finish line without walking.

As we made our way through the neighborhood, I shared with him a story about a friend of mine from college. I'd met Shannon in physical education class my freshman year at Grove City College. We became friends through our mutual love of running and would go on long runs around the college together. One interesting aspect of her running style was that whenever we came to a hill, she would always choose that point to push herself the hardest, often breaking into a sprint. I was always in awe of her strength and determination to do that.

I shared this with my son as we ran down a big hill, hoping to provide him with a little extra motivation for our impending ascent. We made it back up to the top of the hill and I congratulated him on a good "first run." I sent him back home after one mile, telling him he'd need to work up his mileage bit by bit.

Recognizing the need to pace myself is a constant struggle. I often wish for immediate answers to prayers, immediate results when I'm trying to teach the kids and parent them through conflicts. I want to reach a certain point in my own maturity and spiritual development without investing in a long season of learning, listening, and waiting.

My faith will never grow, deepen, or fully mature without training and learning to pace myself. Just like I knew my son should not try to run more than a mile on his first run, I can't expect to reach a certain point in my faith without gradually building up to it. Spending time with God each day must become a habit and priority. Leaning on Him more and more throughout the day, talking with Him through prayer, and going to Him with my concerns and decisions and struggles must become natural responses. A runner learns how to run with the proper stride along with specific breathing techniques. A person with a deep and real faith learns to trust wholeheartedly in God by memorizing and meditating on Scripture, frequent Bible study, and daily (throughout the day) prayer.

Step-by-step and moment-by-moment, I grow when I am tested. I'm reminded not to question it, not to balk at my challenges or my places of pain, but to press on. I pace myself through the difficulties and I learn to lean not on my own understanding but to trust more and more in Him:

> Trust in the Lord with all your heart, and lean not on your own understanding; In all your ways acknowledge Him, and He shall direct your paths (Proverbs 3:5-6).

71. Come

> "Come to Me, all you who labor and are heavy laden, and I will give you rest. Take My yoke upon you and learn from Me, for I am gentle and lowly in heart, and you will find rest for your souls. For My yoke is easy and My burden is light" (Matthew 11:28-30 NKJV).

The weight of the jogging stroller with a baby on board was a burden. I wished right from the first step that I could run hands-free. Every stride was extra effort and every lap grew more and more tiresome. After about two miles, my wonderful husband flagged me down. He was already entertaining the other four kids and offered to take the baby with the others over to the playground. This way I could finish running without the stroller.

"Yes! That would be wonderful!" I told him, and the minute I was running again, I immediately felt the lightness of running without that burden. I could swing my arms again and there was no extra weight to carry. This was how running was meant to be. I was meditating on how I should respond to these words in Matthew that Jesus spoke.

First, He said, "*Come.*" I need to come to Him in all my weakness when I am weary and burdened, and He promises to give me rest. Come just as I am - He is not expecting me to be perfect. He welcomes me in my disfigured, sin-stained state and offers me comfort and healing. He offers rest from the exhausting efforts of trying to make it on my own.

"Take my yoke"

Then He instructs me to take up His yoke. The burden He gives me to carry is manageable, never exceeding what I can handle. He wants me to learn from the example that He set for me. My own self-imposed yokes are heavier than His. I try hard on my own and always fall short. Only when I come to terms with this and set aside my own interests, agendas, priorities, and earthly idols can my focus be completely on Him. Then the burden is lifted and I am free.

"Learn from Me"

I need to learn Jesus' ways for He is gentle and humble in heart. He isn't a cruel teacher waiting to reprimand me for my mistakes. He is patient, gently urging me in the way I should go. He gives me so much freedom to make decisions on my own, and yet the best choice I can ever make is to relinquish my will to Him.

"My burden is light"

Jesus is familiar with the heaviness that this world imposes on me because He experienced it all Himself. He suffered just as I suffer (and far worse). He was brought to tears on many occasions and to His knees in desperation. We still must carry burdens of suffering, illness, loss, and sorrow, but He will walk through these valleys with us. He will give us the will, strength, and courage to carry on. Indeed, He will carry us through them, one step at a time.

Daily I will come to Him, handing over my burden and trusting Him with the things I cannot handle on my own. I've felt my burdens gently lifted many a time. It's how life was meant to be lived.

72. Productive

"Let us not become weary in doing good, for at
the proper time we will reap a harvest
if we do not give up" (Galatians 6:9).

Throughout the winter, I long for spring to come and then suddenly it's here. Plants that were dead for so many months begin to show signs of life again as the spring weather warms the soil. They have endured many weeks of freezing temperatures, frosts, and heavy rains but finally, in spite of the pressures and challenges, they begin to flourish again.

My husband invests hours in planning out and planting a garden every year. Watching our garden plants go from dormancy or tiny seedlings to the harvest is a lengthy and arduous process. For so long there is doubt. Will they survive? Will there be anything to show for all this effort?

Don't grow weary…

This message reverberates in my mind when I contemplate the hard work we put into our flower and veggie gardens. We pull weeds, till the soil to make room for many new seedlings, and then plant the tiny seedlings in neat rows. Paul's message from Galatians reminds me of my need to tend my faith daily, to pull up any encroaching weeds, and to guard it carefully with a covering of prayer.

In due season, I will reap. I will not give up, though it's tempting at times to allow life to swallow up my resolve and my hope. All good things take time and I must never grow weary of doing good. The harvest will come.

73. A Prize-Worthy Life

A win is always exciting to watch. We let my oldest son stay up to watch an NFL game one Christmas evening. It was a nail-biting victory, and the home team was playing from behind for the entire game. There was great uncertainty up until the final seconds whether the home team would win or lose the game. When the winner is the underdog, has to undergo a great trial, or come back from a great deficit, it makes the win more glorious.

First Corinthians 9:24 says, "Do you not know that in a race all the runners run, but only one gets the prize? Run in such a way as to get the prize." What does it mean to live a prize-worthy life? I pondered that once as we battled our way through another round of sickness over the Christmas holidays. There were moments I was discouraged and in despair, along with fatigued from lack of sleep. I experienced moments when the strength to keep going wasn't my own but came straight from the Lord. This was a time already heavy-laden with emotion, as holidays often are, reliving past Christmases, and thinking about those who are no longer with us.

How, Lord, can I keep my head held high when it seems like the odds are stacked against me? How can I race forward for that coveted prize when I feel like I can hardly place one foot in front of the other? How can I maintain the motivation required to press on, and not give up or give in to discouragement?

Psalm 119:32 in the Contemporary Amplified Version states, "I will [not merely walk, but] run the way of Your commandments, when You give me a heart that is willing." I don't have what it takes on my own. God gives me the "heart that is willing." He gives me exactly what I need, when I need it. He imparts the desire to run, not just walk. He enables me to overcome my fatigue, grief, and greatest struggles, giving me the desire to "win."

"Practice what you have learned and received and heard and seen in me, and model your way of living on it, and the God of peace (of untroubled, undisturbed well-being) will be with you" (Philippians 4:9 AMPC). I love how the Amplified version interprets this verse. His peace offers us "untroubled, undisturbed well-being." This kind of peace isn't shaken by the trials we go through. It is enduring.

I long to live a life worthy of the prize. With each new day, may we all find hope in the One who offers hope in our darkest hour and may we desire to live a life that is truly prize-worthy.

74. Great Expectations

"In the morning, Lord, You hear my voice;
in the morning I lay my requests before You
and wait expectantly" (Psalm 5:3).

My daughter ran to me with great urgency in her eyes and held her hand up to my face. "I got a cut, Mama!" I sighed because it was only about the fifth one in two days. I held up her hand to my lips and gave the injured finger (barely a scrape on it) a big kiss. "Better?" I asked her. She smiled her little grin and ran off.

No parent likes to see their dear ones suffer any kind of pain, but sometimes they need to go through painful situations so they can become stronger. The amount of pain I could tolerate as a child has been magnified exponentially after going through five childbirths. When things don't work out exactly as I like them to, that's when I experience real growth.

If there's one thing I've been working on, it's my prayer life. I don't ever want to come across as someone who makes it all sound easy because it's not, yet I don't want to sound like it's impossible, for that's not true either. For me, not only finding the time to pray but finding the time when I'm not completely exhausted or when my mind isn't going in a million different directions is serious work. I am not alone when my heart is seeking the Lord, for then He helps me do what I thought was impossible.

My ideas and concepts of what prayer is, the reasons to pray, and benefits of prayer have all evolved over the past three decades of life. Moving from simplistic, request-driven childhood prayers to the meatier prayers of a seasoned and trial-tested Christian woman has taken some time. There are many days I still feel like I'm in the infancy stages of my prayer life, but I have come so far.

It's difficult for me not to pray with my own agenda in mind. I remind myself that it would be like calling a friend on the phone and only talking about myself and then hanging up. No, prayer is a conversation and I must listen as much if not more than I talk.

Prayer is a lot more than submitting our "wish list" to God every day and hoping for immediate affirmative answers. Prayer is a conversation as we draw near to Him. It is a means of discerning His heart and will. It's a time to confess our shortcomings and sins, to receive His forgiveness and grace, and to thank Him for all the blessings He gives us.

I love the wise words of Proverbs 30:8-9: ". . . give me neither poverty nor riches, but give me only my daily bread . . . ." Give me exactly what I need for today, Lord, which is how Jesus taught us to pray: "give us this day our daily bread" (Matthew 6:11). When we have more than we need, we don't need God as much.

He has promised to give us what we need. It's often a matter of reminding ourselves that what we need and what we think we need are sometimes diametrically opposed. Sometimes it's enough to know that he cares as I follow the Bible's instructions: "I waited patiently for the Lord; He turned to me and heard my cry" (Psalm 40:1). I will not grow weary of laying my requests before the Lord, never giving up hope while I expect great things.

75. Made from Scratch

I was flipping through cookbooks for an hour with my oldest daughter Reese. We'd been to the library and her passionate interest these days is helping out in the kitchen. Now when we go to the library, she checks out some cookbooks to look through and try new recipes. I love that she's so excited to learn the art of cooking and am always happy for her help when I am preparing meals.

As we looked for a new recipe to try, I got a little frustrated with some of the books. Many assumed that the kids won't want to measure, prep, or take the time to make things from scratch, so they called for a box of cake mix, canned or packaged veggies or fruit, or pre-made dough.

As I was standing at the counter one afternoon grating butternut squash from our garden for some squash fritters, I was thinking about this and about how much better things taste when we make them from scratch. People always notice and appreciate it when we take the extra time to cook something from scratch. The flavor is more intense, the nutrition is more complete and healthful, and it's an overall better experience when we have the time and ingredients available. It takes a little more elbow grease to grate a butternut squash than to buy it already prepared, but the results are always worth it.

The same is true for my faith walk and relationship with the Lord. There really is no adequate "shortcut" to grow my faith. There are no "pre-prepared" Scripture readings or ready-made prayer requests. I can't forge lasting and meaningful relationships by posting photos and clicking the like function on Facebook, I can't have a deep and meaningful relationship with God if I only send up text-length prayers to Him and only read my Bible in bits and pieces. I must get in there and be willing to get "sweaty." I've got to push myself to new limits beyond my comfort zone. I've got to work at it, not skipping any steps, putting all my strength into my relationship with Him. And then, when difficult times come, which they will, I'll have a strong foundation to fall back on.

My son Carter and I recently read the story of Jonah at bedtime. I noticed one verse in particular that directly relates to this concept: "In my distress I cried out to the Lord and He heard me; out of the darkness God heard my voice" (Jonah 2:2).

When we take the time to invest ourselves and cultivate

a close and meaningful relationship with the Lord, it becomes an automatic response to turn to Him in difficult times. We can rest assured that He hears us and knows when we struggle, when we doubt, and when we need Him most. He's not a God who turns His back on us in our darkest hours. I've experienced this firsthand many times over the course of my life, but especially over the last few years.

Faith is a step-by-step, life-long process. It's the perfect example of something that is "made from scratch." There are no shortcuts or alternate routes. There is one path to a real and complete relationship with God and He gives us all the instructions, the "recipe" if you will, in His Word.

76. Weary

"The Sovereign Lord has given me his words
of wisdom, so that I know how to comfort the
weary. Morning by morning he wakens me and
opens my understanding to his will"
(Isaiah 50:4 NLT).

The heavy smell of an early morning spring rain wafted in through my open windows. I could hear the drops pitter-pattering on the roof as I sat in my rocking chair, rocking the baby back to sleep. Once she was in her crib again, I wandered over to a chair by the window in my bedroom and just sat there looking out with Bible in hand. I was amazed how verdant the spring leaves and the grass were with that fresh coating of rain. Just a few weeks before, the trees had no leaves at all.

How sweetly the birds all sang to each other in the trees, the new leaves rustling in the gentle breeze. I often overlook so much of this, but on that day, my senses were tuned in to all that was around me. I was glad for the chance to have a few quiet moments with God, enjoying the beauty of His creation before my busy day began. My whole perspective on the day is vastly improved when I have a chance to focus my attention and heart on Him first, before I get into everything else that vies for my time for the rest of my waking hours. In the morning, more than any other time, my senses are tuned in to Him and what He might want to tell me.

Life is a step-by-step journey, requiring great determination. It is by no means a sprint race. I see many of my fellow sojourners in struggles resembling mine. God gives me opportunities along the way to offer words of comfort and encouragement. The beauty of a new day reminds me that in spite of our weariness, there is hope. Despite our trials, there is reason to press on and continue to trust in God's plan for us. When I listen for Him in the morning, He directs my path and gives me words of wisdom, Though I am weary, I find strength and purpose in Him.

77. Soaring

I have never seen an eagle fly. Yes, I've seen them on TV and I've actually seen eagles in the wild, but they were sitting on a nest. I can only imagine how majestic these birds must be out in the wild, rising on a wind current and swooping down with the next. When God gives, He gives us the best. He doesn't make us soar like a sparrow, or a pigeon. No, He chose the eagle.

The closest thing to soaring I've ever experienced was when I did a ropes course with my husband on our anniversary. We were high up in the trees, walking precariously across narrow rope and wooden bridges. At one point, we were up on a platform, and the only way across was to step out, off the safety of the platform, and free fall until the slack in the rope harness pulled us swinging across to another tree. It was terrifying, something I never thought I could or would do, being afraid of heights. That feeling was amazing when the free fall ended and the rope swung me over to safety.

What a reassurance it is for me to know this about God's character, for in my weakest hour, in my times of failure, doubt, and despair, God is quietly waiting to renew and restore my strength and allow me to soar.

Soaring requires heavy-duty trust. We have to trust that

our wings will hold us up and allow us to steer in the direction we want to go. We also have to trust in the wind (God), something and someone we cannot see, that it (He) will carry us along.

I think again of that favorite passage in Isaiah 40:31: "But those who hope in the Lord will renew their strength. They will soar on wings like eagles; they will run and not grow weary, they will walk and not be faint."

The certainty of God's presence in my life allows me to soar. Through Him, I can mount up on wings that are strong and trustworthy. With God's strength, I can run and not grow weary. Can you also sense Him in these ways? Do you long for this infusion of strength, and the ability to transcend your trials and weaknesses? Ask Him to help you. He is waiting to hear from you if you will only put aside your pride and ask.

Chapter 14
A Vital Necessity

I never knew how difficult packing for a trip could be. The kids were ecstatic when my husband and I told them the news of our upcoming vacation to the beach. All we could think of was the amount of work it would require and the grueling ten hours it would take to get there with five kids in the car. They were quite excited to help with the packing, and I told them they could help get their clothes packed in their own suitcases. Even with little lists of what to pack, it was amazing to see the things they thought were priorities to bring versus what they really needed.

My daughter Reese filled her suitcase with books, Sienna filled hers with baby dolls and all of the dolls' clothes. When we started to pack some snacks for the car, Lawson ran to the pantry, grabbed the snack bag we had started to fill, and began throwing in fistfuls of candy. After about three trips for more, I stopped him in his tracks: "No more candy! We don't need to bring candy!" He was disappointed and dejected. For him, this was an indispensible item and vacation would not be a success without it.

When I wake up each morning, how do I "pack" and prepare for the day ahead? I give myself a mental pep-talk, trying to be positive and excited about keeping my kids fed, clothed, clean, and alive for another 14-hour day. All too often, however, I'm running out of steam by the time breakfast is over. My bags are often full of "candy." I don't adequately prepare for the day by fueling up on God's word. I burn through my reserves quickly and hit a wall.

When I think about the Lord's Prayer, the phrase "give us this day our daily bread" takes on new meaning. Jesus referred to Himself as the Bread of life, and for good reason. If I'm trying to get through life by energizing myself on things that aren't sustaining, I'm going to burn out and won't arrive at my destination adequately prepared. God wants me to incorporate Him throughout my entire day. His presence should permeate every minute, His Word should reverberate in my mind as I parent, helping me to build and nurture relationships in my home. Do I behave as though I *need* God? Or is He merely an afterthought, something I squeeze in when I have a few free minutes at the end of my day? Do I treat God as my vital necessity? How often have I experienced a vital need? What does this even truly mean?

I draw back on a memory of watching swallowtail caterpillars to better explain my need for God. Over the years, we've collected many from our garden and watched them transform from creamy white eggs the size of a period into fat caterpillars. The day my kids found the eggs on some fennel growing in our garden, they were absolutely ecstatic. We never tire of watching

Reese and a newly-hatched Swallowtail butterfly

their dramatic transformation over the period of just a few weeks.

Their success in reaching their glorious butterfly stage is fully dependent on just one thing when they are a caterpillar: food. If the mother doesn't lay her eggs in the right place, they cannot flourish. A caterpillar's entire existence is elegantly simple: eat, grow, and molt, eat, grow, and molt – and then *transform*.

I wish I had that kind of focus so I could know exactly what I need and then seek it, not swayed by any outside influences. I wish I had that instinctual path going through methodical stages until I reached full maturity. But life is far more complex than that for you and me. From the time we are born, we are pummeled with a myriad of decisions. At first, our parents help us sort through these, but eventually we have to learn and do it for ourselves.

Often we can make it far without the thing we truly need. Some may say they live out their entire lives with great success and contentment entirely on their own terms. Just as a diet of junk food would leave me devoid of the nutrition I need to thrive, a life lived without God leaves me in a place of great need and unfulfilled longing, never being able to live up to my full potential.

I cling to God as my vital necessity, realizing more and more how poorly I make decisions on my own, as well as how much I need His direction to survive and thrive. How quick I am to judge, get angry, and point out faults in others while ignoring my own. I lose patience and act selfishly. I also lose sight of what's truly important and instead begin to feast on things that have no spiritual calories.

God, give me the focus and instinct to always go back to You. I long for you and your Word. Let me seek You out each day as food for my soul. When we wholeheartedly search for Him, we find Him: "Then [with a deep longing] you will seek Me and require Me [as a vital necessity] and [you will] find Me when you search for Me with all your heart" (Jeremiah 29:13 AMPC).

78. Like a Well-Watered Garden

I took the baby out for a 45-minute run in her jogging

stroller the other day, right in the peak of the afternoon heat and sunshine. As I finished and trudged up the driveway, I was aching for a cold, refreshing drink. I had an intense need at that moment and knew it would only be satisfied when I drank some water.

I'm reminded that life is fragile when I look back over the journey I've been on in the last few years. Like that refreshing gulp of water I take after an exhausting run, I grab hold of the Lord even more tightly during times of peril. As good as that is, He desires even more, reminding me that the need is always there. I need Him every day, as much on good days as I do on the bad, as I need water every day to thrive and survive. He will *always* guide me, as the words of Isaiah 58:11 remind me:

> The Lord will guide you always, He will satisfy your needs in a sun-scorched land and will strengthen your frame. You will be like a well-watered garden, like a spring whose waters never fail.

He makes me like a well-watered garden and will not fail me! I can choose to live out my faith in two ways. In the first, I wait until I'm wilting and withering away, too weary of going it alone, then turning back to God. The second is that I draw deeply from the well of His limitless spring of life-giving water every day. I recognize my need and inability to manage on my own, relying on Him completely. He satisfies and strengthens me. He will not fail.

79. The Fountain

> How precious is your unfailing love, O God! All
> humanity finds shelter in the shadow of your
> wings. You feed them from the abundance of
> your own house, letting them drink from your
> river of delights. For you are the fountain of life,
> the light by which we see (Psalm 36:7-9 NLT).

I never realized until recently how many beautiful fountains there are in the city of Pittsburgh. They are tucked away in places I have driven past dozens of times, but missed seeing them

Carter and Reese visiting one of Pittsburgh's many fountains

because I was in a hurry. As the kids and I traipsed around the city one morning for a tour and history lesson about these fountains, my eyes were opened to their beauty and the way they enhance the landscape for everyone.

I never stopped to think about fountains much before, but I further understood the calming and healing properties of water as we toured. Its sound in the midst of the noisy city is amazing. Several of the fountains were so loud that they drowned out almost all other sounds. Fountains have a quasi-magical property of spurting water that then reappears in an infinite and endless cycle of beauty.

All this coincides with biblical references to fountains. The Lord is described as "the fountain of life." He pours out life for us day-in and day-out. It flows forth from Him in an endless gush of beauty that reveals truth to us. His awe-inspiring presence drowns out the distractions of everyday life. When we draw near to Him, we are enveloped in the abundance of His love for us.

I stand in the presence of the greatest Fountain known to man. Here I find a *river of delights*. He shines forth the *light by which I see.*

80. Something Old, Something New

After years of having a few dingy old pillows on our couch, my husband purchased some new ones for me for as a gift. It felt great to have something new to look at since there isn't a whole lot in my house that's "new and fresh" these days. Just a few weeks after receiving the pillows, our baby spit up all over one. We ran it through the wash only to have it get completely torn to shreds by our washing machine, which leaves me with just one new pillow.

Around the same time, we painted our dining room, which we had intended to do for eight months. I walked out one day to see Lawson, perched at Carter's school desk, coloring with a pen on the newly-painted wall.

Why is it that nothing new ever lasts? You may respond because we have a house full of kids. That's certainly part of it, but when I stop to think about it, nothing new ever stays new, and this extends far beyond my couch cushions or paint on the wall.

If I'm counting on that "new" feeling to last, I'm going to be regularly disappointed. If I keep looking to the material things around me for meaning and purpose, I will always end up discouraged. If I'm expecting anything in this life to remain constant and unchanging, I'll be chasing after the wind all of my days. Peter wrote in his epistle, "All men are like grass and all their glory is like the flowers of the field. The grass withers and the flowers fall but the Word of the Lord stands forever" (1 Peter 1:24-25).

Does this then mean I am to remove all expectations of good things to come in this life? What should my response be when I consider the temporal nature of all things? Part of the answer is in another verse: ". . . provide purses for yourselves that will not wear out, a treasure in heaven that will never fail, . . . for where your treasure is, there your heart will be also" (Luke 12: 33-34).

That's the kind of treasure I hope for, the kind I want to invest in and count on. It may take great patience and perseverance to look forward to a treasure that is beyond this earth, but the wait will be well worth it. While I'm here, I ask God to grant me the courage to focus first on the things that last. May He keep me from dwelling on disappointment when my earthly comforts and treasures are taken from me, but to turn to Him instead. May He fill me with great hope and expectation, transcending what is seen now and remembering to focus more on what is temporarily unseen but promised to me again and again.

May He give me eyes to see every morning when I awake that "the steadfast love of the Lord never ceases, His mercies never come to an end; they are new every morning" (Lamentations 3:22-23).

81. The Lifeguard

"And behold, I am with you and will keep watch
over you with care, take notice of you wherever
you may go" (Genesis 28:15 AMPC).

He walked with a confident swagger wearing fluorescent orange shorts and a red cutoff t-shirt that were dead giveaways to his profession. Even off duty, he wore these as a badge of honor and rightly so. His job was to protect and save lives and what could be more honorable than that? Emblazoned on the back of his shirt was one word – lifeguard.

There is something comforting about entering into the tumultuous surf knowing that a lifeguard is watching nearby. The ocean is unpredictable and powerful, and filled with many potential hazards. I am certainly not qualified to do an ocean rescue if it involves anything beyond the shallow surf. I've seen a rescue before as the flailing victim was being carried out to sea. I watched the lifeguard swim through the same water, unafraid and with a single purpose in mind – to save that person.

Life is like an awesome ocean, full of potential hazards, rip currents, and pummeling waves that can knock even the strongest people off their feet. I am ever thankful for the Lifeguard, who is on duty 24/7, looking for anyone who needs to be rescued. I've been caught up in rugged surf before and have felt His strong grip on my arm pulling me to safety. I know my inadequacies when it comes to negotiating these troubled waters on my own. There is someone much greater than I who cares about my well-being, safety, life, and my very soul. He will not turn away from me, will never leave or forsake me, His watchful eye is ever upon me: "For the Son of Man came to seek and save those who are lost" (Luke 19:10 NLT).

82. A Walk with the Lord

She gazed with wide-eyed wonder as I pushed her stroller down the street. There were many new and wonderful things to look at, most beyond her comprehension. She seemed not to mind, for her eight-month-old mind was not at all concerned. She had not a moment of worry or distrust in the one who was propelling her along on this new adventure. She was along for the ride and riding in trust.

As I reflected on that scene, it reminded me in so many ways of my walk, or how I should walk with the Lord. As we stroll our way through life together, there are many things that I cannot comprehend. He urges me not to worry or fear but to steadfastly hold on to His truths and promises to me.

Together we walk a path of great uncertainty and that is what comforts me. Though plans I make often fall through, He knows the plans He has for me. Though my ability to understand often falters, though life is flooded with a great many sorrows and pains, I am carried along by the Lifter of my soul, my Rock and my Fortress.

And so a new day begins. I strap myself in for the ride, eyes wide open for what He might teach me today. I am ready for and unafraid of whatever life brings because He is with me: "But you, Lord, are a shield around me, my glory, the One who lifts my head high" (Psalm 3:3).

83. A Dozen Yellow Roses

As I stood in line at the grocery store, I watched a little girl in front of me. She was quite taken with a display of different colored roses. She grabbed a bouquet and bowed her whole face right down into them, breathing in deeply. "They smell so good!" she exclaimed. Her mother, who hadn't been intending to buy 12 yellow roses that day, smiled and put them in the cart.

There is something special about flowers. You don't ever see bouquets of artificial flowers on display at the store. Even though they only last a few days, people still buy live flowers, preferring the real thing over the artificial because the latter can never duplicate that kind of delicate beauty.

There's a space in our hearts that yearns for the real. We may try to fill it with other things, things that give us temporary fulfillment or joy, but they just don't compare. My soul yearns for the supernatural and my heart craves the eternal God I was made to worship. I plunge my face into a cluster of fake flowers and breathe in deep, but alas there is no fragrance! I try to find lasting joy in the temporal things of this world but nothing can compare to the joy I find in the Lord.

The act of true worship gives off an intoxicating and alluring aroma. God desires it, and shouldn't we that much more?

> But thanks be to God, who in Christ always leads us in triumphal procession, and through us spreads the fragrance of the knowledge of him everywhere (2 Corinthians 2:14 ESV).

84. The Need for Light

One day I noticed something strange with the two large flower pots sitting on either side of my front door. I had recently planted some mums in the pots to replace the fading flowers of summer. The mums had not yet bloomed when I planted them and looked almost identical. A couple weeks later the mums began to slowly open and eventually were in full bloom. There was a marked difference between the two, for one pot received a few extra hours of sunlight throughout the day, while the other pot was closer to the house and thus more shaded.

The flowers in the pot receiving more sunlight were brilliantly colored and had larger, fuller blooms. The flowers in the more shaded pot were dull-colored and much smaller. Some of them had begun to die off already while the flowers in the sunnier pot were still going strong. I was amazed how just a few hours of light every day could make that much of a difference. It literally changed the character of the flowers and impacted their ability to grow and flourish.

Light allows us to see things but it also brings beauty and causes things to flourish. It's interesting that in the creation story, the first thing God created was light. It's also of note how often Jesus is referred to in the Bible as the light: "Once again, Jesus spoke to the people and said, 'I am the light of the world. Whoever follows Me will never walk in the darkness, but will have the light of life'" (John 8:12).

I have a choice to accept and walk in the light or to walk in darkness. Ephesians 5:8-9 says "Walk as children of light, for the fruit of the light consists in all goodness, righteousness, and truth." My life would not be the same without the kind of light God brings to it. I would be a stunted, withering, half-dead version of myself without the beauty and strength He infuses me with each and every day that I live and breathe. Unlike the weatherman who predicts sunny skies on a day that turns out to be cloud-covered, the Light He brings is steady and an absolute certainty.

Chapter 15
She Will not Fall

"God is within her, she will not fall; God will
help her at break of day" (Psalm 46:5).

I have no strength to withstand even the most routine day
without God. During an exceptionally difficult day, I happened
upon Psalm 46:5 and the words resonated with me. The promises
of God seem shallow at times when I am going through a particularly rough patch. I know that He is with me even in my storms.
In my head I know this to be true but my heart still aches. I long
for my journey to grow easier not harder. I would like a path
where there are no stumbling blocks or barricades in my way, one
that is straight and easy. This verse reminds me that though I may
trip repeatedly and wind up on my face in the dirt, He will not
let me fall.

I have had, and still have, some remarkable women in my
life, women whose own faith has been a motivation and inspiration to me. They have showed me the meaning of this verse by the
way they lived and still live their lives. They demonstrated for me
that belief in God does not exempt me from problems or pain but
that He meets me at the start of each new day, ready to help me
through whatever I am facing. Faith in God isn't deepened when
things suddenly turn around and go my way. My faith is deepened
as I walk through valley after valley by keeping my eyes turned

upwards to Him.

It is a temptation to dwell on my losses, to look at the cliff walls rising on either side of me and feel discouraged. It is in those moments when I sense God's presence and His provision for me most powerfully. He has not left me here alone and He walks with me in my struggles. Though life may change, people may leave me, and difficulties stand in my way, still I will not fall.

85. A Grandmother's Legacy

If there is anyone who nurtured in me a growing desire to know God, it was my grandmother. I began to get a taste of the greatness of God by spending time with this precious woman on a regular basis. There was rarely a time I was with her that God was not mentioned. He was as much a part of her life as was breakfast, lunch, and dinner. Her relationship with the Lord was real and vibrant, and I always walked away from my times with her thinking, "I want to know the Lord like that."

When I was a young child and stayed at her house, she sang me to sleep at night with old hymns like *The Old Rugged Cross* and *Jesus, Jesus, Jesus, Sweetest Name I Know*. She awakened daily at 5 AM and jumped on her little exercise trampoline, read her Bible, and prayed. She cared for her physical, emotional, and spiritual needs with devout dedication and because of this, she truly moved mountains in the almost 95 years she lived here on this earth.

My mom gave me a letter she found among my grandmother's possessions after she passed away in 2013, a letter she had written to our whole family in 1984. I have read and re-read it many times since she gave it to me. It brings my grandmother back to me, like I am sitting down and having a conversation with her as we did so many times in the past. I want to share a portion of that letter because it is such an encouragement and points me in the right direction when I'm veering off track:

> *You need to be "walking in the light of His word" daily, not just sometimes or somehow but consistently. It means*

not being afraid to face self-denial that His highest may be attained. It means self-discipline of thought, word and deed, disciplined by the living word of God. All of this is not a chore, but a joy, a joy only He can give as a result of the fullness of His presence.

*Live each day as though this be **the** day. Learn to love and be considerate of all men. Real love — God's love from a sincere heart for even the meanest of creatures — breaks down all barriers and paves the way for men to hear of the source of such love. Remember, we are to love the unlovely.*

Don't live for self. If you do, that's all you will have and you won't enjoy that as you think you will. Consider the lost and never stop praying for them and seeking to reach them by every means at your command as long as you live. I hope I have been a testimony to you in this.

Don't wait for tomorrow to begin living for Him today — wherever you are, whatever you are doing — this is His will for you. In school, teaching, the office, leisure time — all can be filled with the joy of knowing He is in control.

You have all been a source of great joy to me — you have no need ever to look back — never waste time doing that — only ahead.

I will not wait for tomorrow. I am looking ahead right now and this motivates me to do the right thing, to live with purpose, and to rejoice in the greatness of God. I am looking forward to the promises God has made to me, to my eternal home in Heaven. I will not dwell in the sadness of yesterday, but will rejoice in each day God gives me to live, to deepen my relationship with Him, and to show His love to others.

I never saw even the tiniest crack in the resolve or firm faith my grandmother possessed. God sustained her for all her years and was her ever-present help.

In 2013, the same year my grandmother passed away, God brought another special woman into my life. I met her when she was a spry 99, feisty, elegant, well-spoken, and ready to share a word of wisdom anytime she had the opportunity. I never expected to forge a friendship with someone like her because so many years separated us as well as different life experiences. Over the months, I grew to know her better through the Bible study we both attended. Something beautiful happened between us; Miss Sally and I became good friends.

Whenever I had the chance to visit her, I was always blessed by her keen wit and sense of humor. God was truly the essence of this woman's being, the fuel that kept her going on a daily basis. She has inspired my children and me in so many ways.

On one visit to her house, the first thing she shared with my children was, "I need to tell you something very important. If there is anything you need, or anything you are worrying about, all you need to do is say, 'Help me, Jesus,' and He will!"

Sally told me many times how she still managed to live at home by herself, even navigating a steep flight of stairs daily to get to her bedroom. She came down the steps in the morning reciting the Lord's Prayer, and she walked back up at night reciting Psalm 23. I asked Sally how she dealt with many difficult situations over the course of her life as she recently celebrated her 103rd birthday! She told me that "God says we must ask, not because He needs to know. He already does; but we need to ask for help in and out of troubles. It's the discipline of asking that forces us to take action and take a step forward in faith."

So many days are spent worrying about things we cannot control, feeling like we cannot get ahead, no matter how hard we try, searching for true meaning and purpose. I always came away from this humble and unassuming woman, re-energized and encouraged beyond measure. The words of Jesus "seek and you shall find" seemed to echo through her house.

Psalm 46:5 often comes to mind after spending time with Sally, for those words truly summarize and describe who she is: "God is within her, she will not fall; God will help her at break of day" (Psalm 46:5).

On one visit, just as we were ready to leave, Miss Sally stopped us and said, "Wait, I have a token I want to give you. It's something that costs nothing but it's worth more than your very life." *What could that be?* I wondered, as we waited for her to pull something out of a drawer. It was a frame with a verse in it: "As for me and my house, we will serve the Lord" (Joshua 24:15). "I don't give these to just anyone. I have to hear from the Holy Spirit to find out who to give them to," she informed us.

That verse from Joshua is oft-quoted and one that, at first glance, we may not think is all that impactful. But when we really think about and apply it, the implications are far-reaching. The same verse also says in the first part, "Choose this day whom you will serve." We are tempted daily to serve so many things other than God. We are also tempted throughout our lives to put all our time and energy into pursuits other than God.

I've been tempted to get caught up in sorrow, regret, and discouragement, all capable of clouding my perspective and distracting me from what ultimately should be my sole purpose in life: serving the Lord. Serve Him first and everything else is superfluous. Serve Him first and everything else will fall in line in due time.

I am thankful for the wise friends and mentors who are in my life to give me these little nudges when I need them. They all help to keep me on track and keep me focused on what my primary goals should be. I am thankful for saints like Sally who can look back over the years and tell me, "This is where you need to focus your energy. This is what will give you the most meaning in your life."

As we turned to leave Sally, we offered our goodbyes along with warm hugs. It was a bittersweet moment whenever we came to the goodbyes. There is something very dear about having a friend who is 103 years old. Each time we parted, we were never certain if we would see each other again. Each day is a precious gift and I know my dear friend will one day soon be gloriously joining her Lord in heaven. Oh, that I would treat all my relationships the same way. If only I would handle each encounter as though it were my last, treat each day as if it were my final one, cherish each breath as the gift it truly is! Knowing Sally has taught

Carter and Miss Sally

me this and has given me this perspective and the chance to love someone who could be taken away at any moment.

86. God Always Wins

I called Sally one day to set up a time to come and visit. As I hung up the phone, these words echoed through my mind, "God always wins." I stood barefoot in my kitchen, looking out the window at my kids splashing in their blow-up pool on the deck. Their laughter permeated the whole yard, their joy at the coolness of the water on an oppressively hot day was undeniable. I looked at the yard as they played. There had been a resurgence of summer, for there had not been a drop of rain for some time. Everything was withered and dry, the grass was dead, and the trees were losing their leaves.

"God always wins," Sally said. What a true statement, yet I don't always live with that mindset. Sally lives with an unquenchable, irrepressible joy in spite of her many pains, seasons of drought, and trials. At 103 years old, she has the vitality of a woman decades younger. Smiles come effortlessly to her lips and words of

154

encouragement bubble out of her. I visit her with the expectation of offering her something but always come away blessed by what she has given.

I once asked Sally what advice she would give to someone who is struggling with faith. "Know Jesus," she said. "Consult Him for a foundation to build and sustain a life of peace. Ask Him to save you from sins big and small. Seek Him and learn to sense His presence. It is a wonderful sensation of peace and joy that young or old can cultivate in Him, a relationship unimaginable!"

It is encouraging to see how real God is to Sally. He has given her a confidence and joy so she can keep on keeping on, even at her advanced age. "God always wins," she had told me, "in spite of the chaos that engulfs this world, along with the pain, trials, and tests. We can be assured of that."

I pray that my victorious lifestyle reflects the truths of God's promises to me. May I walk in the great victory I know I have over sin, death, sorrow, and pain, and live out my years in that irrepressible joy only He can offer. James 1:2 reminds me to "count it all joy" and John 7:38 (BSB) reminds me of what is possible even in the midst of my droughts: "To the one who believes in Me, it is just as the Scripture has said: 'Streams of living water will flow from within him.'"

A new day dawns, and it is impossible for me to overlook the ways that God is with me. How can that be? With so many bad things happening, this would be the perfect time to cast blame on God or to turn away. If God is good and truly cares for me, why would He have allowed all of this to happen? I have been tested. I have suffered and experienced losses beyond my imagination. I also never knew the riches of His greatness as I do now. By having so many loved ones taken away, my sense of His presence has been heightened and my faith has been deepened.

Having an immovable foundation has never been so vital to me as during these recent years. He has placed amazing women-of-faith in my life to constantly remind me of His plan for me. I will not fall prey to discouragement and depression. I will not fail because He's established in me a solid rock foundation that will not crumble or be moved. I will not fall because He is with me at the break of each new day.

Author's note: *As we went to press, Sarah "Sally" Brooks passed away on February 23, 2018 at the age of 103. Thank you, my inspirational mentor and dear friend. You will be greatly missed. Heaven rejoices at your passage into eternity to be in the presence of your loving Father.*

Chapter 16
Finish Well

There is a race I've run about 14 times over the past 18 years, called The Great Race. It's a 10K run through the city of Pittsburgh and about 10,000 runners participate every September. Anyone who has run the race bemoans the difficult fourth mile, a steady uphill that lasts for a mile and seems like it will never end. At that point in the race, fatigue is already building and it's tempting to give up. If runners can press through that difficult mile, the final portion of the race is all downhill.

In 2017, The Great Race was particularly difficult because the temperatures soared to near 90 degrees on race day. As I ran, I thought back on previous races I had run, several of them with my friend who is now in prison and one with my brother, who has been gone now for more than two years. The sun scorched down on me and my body poured sweat. The heat was intense, sapping my energy even more quickly than usual. The physical pain of running on such a hot day, intermingled with the pain of loved ones lost, caused me to ask in my heart, "How will I get through this, God? I feel as if I'm trapped in a perpetual fourth mile."

I've been running all my life, starting with those childhood races around the playground to this mini-marathon I now run. I am balancing my responsibilities of raising five children while grieving my brother and my mother. Have I adequately trained for this race? Will I somehow manage to make it to the finish line? His answer comes to me between my gasps for air, "You must fight the good fight. You must not give up hope."

Life was not meant to be easy, and He certainly never promised that it would be. In fact, He assures us that we will face many trials, but reminds us that He has overcome the world: "I have told you all this so that you may have peace in me. Here on earth you will have many trials and sorrows. But take heart, because I have overcome the world" (John 16:33 NLT).

Keep on going. Press on in the faith that you have fallen back on so many times before: "I press on toward the goal to win the prize for which God has called me heavenward in Christ Jesus" (Philippians 3:14), and "Trust in the Lord with all your heart and lean not on your own understanding" (Proverbs 3:5).

I find Him like an oasis in the desert. He offers me water for my parched soul. I am running in the greatest race possible, one that will lead me to my promised final home. I know that I will not be stuck in the fourth mile forever. I know there is an end in sight. I press on towards glory and towards a prize that will last. I press on despite the pain, doubt, and despair.

Paul wrote in 2 Timothy 4:7-8, "I have fought the good fight, I have finished the race, I have kept the faith. Now there is in store for me the crown of righteousness, which the Lord, the righteous Judge, will award to me on that day—and not only to me, but also to all who have longed for his appearing."

The Apostle Paul was a good example of pressing on through trials. He experienced hardship yet his words don't seem to reflect that. If there is anything we can learn from Paul, it is that *his memory was short where his sufferings were concerned.* He did not hold on to the pains of life. His eyes were always on the prize and final goal. He knew and believed in the promises of God and he pursued them with all of his might. Without question, he showed us how to finish well.

87. Intensity

I love watching my kids because everything they do is done with great intensity. They aren't afraid to throw themselves entirely into whatever pursuit they fancy with no fear of failing.

My athletic son Lawson is no exception.

"Did you see my new soccer shoes?" When he was two, he lived to wear his soccer shoes from the minute he finished breakfast in the morning until we peeled them off his wet and sweaty little feet at night. One night at dinner, not only was he wearing the cleats, but he also insisted on clutching an orange soccer ball in his right arm while trying to eat. This kid is intensely devoted to his sports, whether it's football, hockey, basketball, or soccer. He loves them all and never stops moving. He would slide open the door in the kitchen after breakfast each morning and proclaim, "It's a nice day out!" (which in toddler speak means, "I'm going outside right now"). It could be raining or be sub-zero temperatures but it didn't matter to him. His one desire was to get out there and play, play, play.

When I think about my walk with the Lord, I long to have the kind of intensity my kids have when it comes to my faith and pursuit of Him. As I delve into Scripture, I see the full measure of His pursuit of me and it is humbling. He relentlessly loves me, won't ever give up on me, and has given everything for me. I read a verse from Isaiah in the Amplified version that speaks to intensity in the Lord's matters:

> And therefore the Lord [earnestly] waits [expecting, looking, and longing] to be gracious to you; and therefore He lifts Himself up, that He may have mercy on you and show loving-kindness to you. For the Lord is a God of justice. Blessed (happy, fortunate, to be envied) are all those who [earnestly] wait for Him, who expect and look and long for Him [for His victory, His favor, His love, His peace, His joy, and His matchless, unbroken companionship]! (Isaiah 30:18).

This speaks to my heart during a time that is emotionally heavy for me. I find blessing when I look and long for Him. He gives to me matchless and unbroken companionship. May we all strive to follow God with an intensity that throws caution to the wind, just like a sprinter racing across the finish line who throws himself forward with his or her last ounce of strength.

88. Grace Upon Grace

I often wonder what kind of parent I am and if I measure up to what I should be. Often I feel discouraged and ready to give up. I am exhausted, but entertained by the antics my kids perform right in front of my very eyes. I revel in their accomplishments only to feel the sting of disappointment when they turn right around and make a bad decision immediately afterwards. More importantly, when my kids don't live up to my hopes and expectations, what is my reaction? When I think about model parenting, I am drawn to the verses in the Bible that describe the love our Heavenly Father bestows on us, His often-wayward children: "See what great love the Father has lavished on us, that we should be called children of God! And that is what we are!" (1 John 3:1).

He lavishes His love on us regardless of the way we behave or how devoted we are (or are not) to Him. He daily gives us good gifts and many of them are taken for granted. It sounds familiar to my own parenting experiences. The difference is that He offers so much more than I ever could to my children. One morning in my devotions, I read a passage from John 1:16: "And from His fullness we have all received, grace upon grace." He is always full to overflowing. His love is boundless, limitless, and unconditional. I love the Amplified translation of the phrase "grace upon grace." It reads instead "spiritual blessing upon spiritual blessing, favor upon favor, and gift heaped upon gift."

How often do we perceive the full measure of His blessings, His favor, and the good gifts He bestows upon us? Do we take notice or are we too busy complaining about the things we don't have?

When I think about the kind of parent I am, rather than looking more to the failings of my children, I need to carefully examine my own failings and identify ways I can point them back to God, their perfect Father. As often as they disappoint me, I disappoint them too, but God will never disappoint. I want to model for them a spirit of gratitude.

We can never truly appreciate all the gifts if we aren't making a conscious effort to see and be thankful for them. Paul wrote in 1 Corinthians 11:23, "The Lord Jesus, on the night He was betrayed, took bread, and when He had given thanks, He broke it and said, 'This is My body, which is for you; do this in remembrance of Me.'"

On the night He was betrayed

On that night when He knowingly and willingly gave Himself up for you and for me, Jesus gave thanks! He was not ignorant of the torture and suffering He would soon endure on our behalf. He knew full well it would all culminate in the most painful death imaginable, with the people He loved so dearly spitting on Him and jeering at Him as He took those last anguished breaths. What did He do in anticipation of all this suffering? *He gave thanks!*

I don't think I can possibly hear the word grace the same way again. When I think about what it means to be a recipient of His grace – and not just once but grace given over and over and over again – I am overwhelmed and thankful beyond measure.

I am grateful for this grace upon grace. He gives me love regardless of my too-often failings. He isn't a God of grudges but One of forgiveness and encouragement.

> But he gives us more grace. That is why Scripture says: "God opposes the proud but shows favor to the humble." . . . Humble yourselves before the Lord, and he will lift you up (James 4:6, 10).

89. Finish Well

"If God is for us, who can be against us?" (Romans 8:31).

Who or what can come between me and the Almighty God? No one and nothing! Psalm 46:1 states, "God is our Refuge and Strength [mighty and impenetrable to temptation], a very present and well-proved help in trouble" (AMPC).

What does it mean to be a well-proved help to us? That phrase is a great reminder that my Savior has been through it all. He faced the same struggles we face, lived through the same trials we go through, felt temptations, hunger, sorrow, fear, persecution, and worry. Yet He has a perfect track record in spite of all this. If there is anyone worthy of taking on our burdens, it's Him.

My course is set and He guides me in the path I should take. I lean on Him and await His guidance and direction. I seek His wisdom daily. God stretches out before me like a vast ocean. I stand at the edge and behold His greatness. This greatness is overwhelming to me and yet I am not afraid. I hear Him calling me in the distance, "Finish well!"

> But my life is worth nothing to me unless I use it for finishing the work assigned me by the Lord Jesus—the work of telling others the Good News about the wonderful grace of God (Acts 20:24 NLT).

Finish well, dear friend, finish well!

Conclusion

I hope you have experienced some of the wonder and greatness of God through these stories and reflections. I also hope this book has given you reason to pause and consider your responses to personal trials and that you have also gained a sense of hope. Despite everything I have been through, I know that God has made me a stronger and more faith-filled person now than I was previously. God has used the deepest valleys to chip away my pride, reduce my self-sufficiency, and make me the person He wants me to be.

It is my prayer that you sense the Lord speaking to your heart too. May He reach down into your places of deepest pain and rescue you. May you embrace Him and trust in His purpose for your life, a life that is precious to Him.

I would enjoy hearing how this book has ministered to you. Please write me at beradsj@gmail.com.

Epilogue

My hands trembled and my heart was heavy as I gripped the steering wheel. I backed my car out of the garage to take Waenyod, my sister-in-law, and Dalis, my beautiful niece, to the airport. We were at the end of an incredible week, a week that had passed by all too quickly. I had waited two years to meet my niece and see my sister-in-law again. What a gift she gave us, bringing an almost two-year-old from Thailand to Pittsburgh. I could never adequately express my gratitude to her for making such an extreme sacrifice to do so.

It was a purely magical experience to finally meet this little "miracle" child. From the minute she walked in the door, there was an irrepressible happiness welling up in my heart. She was enchanting in every way. Seeing her first encounter with snow, sharing in her second birthday celebration, and living life with her for a week was so joyful. I could see my brother in her through her sense of independence and adventure and love of activity. She took to the snow like a seasoned pro, and was often the last man standing when everyone else had tired and wanted to come back inside. One of the English words she had picked up by the end of this week was "again" from the many times she wanted to sled down our hill in the backyard.

It was a poignant moment as I got closer and closer to the airport and a goodbye I was dreading. Their flight would take them home – back to the other side of the world. It was difficult for me to let them go and watch them walk away. They brought me such a sense of family that I have missed these past two-and-a-half years since my brother passed away. They rekindled a sense of hope and togetherness along with an appreciation for the many ways God has truly blessed me. It took me back to the coastline, overlooking a vast body of water that stretched farther than the eye could see. It reminded me of that sense of God's greatness and my own inadequacy to comprehend all that He is and all that He *is doing*. Clearly He is at work in my life and has a plan much greater than my own. Can I trust Him to see it through to completion?

God has opened my eyes to a world much larger than what I ever imagined it could be through all this. I never would have envisioned that things would be this way, never would have expected my family to look like this, but He has a way of stretching us far beyond what we would ever choose.

In the few minutes of quiet as I drove home alone from the airport, I tearfully reflected back on my life. The one thing that stuck out in my mind the most was the reminder that so many "things" of this world are fleeting and unimportant, but the greatest gift any of us can give or receive is love. I reflected on the verses in 1 Corinthians 13, the love chapter:

Love is patient and kind.

Love is not jealous or boastful or proud or rude.

It does not demand its own way.

It is not irritable, and it keeps no record of being wronged.

It does not rejoice about injustice but rejoices whenever the truth wins out.

Love never gives up, never loses faith, is always hopeful, and endures through every circumstance.

When I was a child, I spoke and thought and reasoned as a child. But when I grew up, I put away childish things. Now we see things imperfectly, like puzzling reflections in a mirror, but then we will see everything with perfect clarity.

All that I know now is partial and incomplete, but then I will know everything completely, just as God now knows me completely.

Three things will last forever—faith, hope, and love—and the greatest of these is love (1 Corinthians 13:4-13).

Carter, Reese, Sienna, Lawson, and Evangeline

Acknowledgments

I am deeply indebted to God for giving me the words for this book. I never would have had any of these insights were it not for the quiet revelations He speaks to me during my long and crazy days. Many people have believed in and encouraged me along the way. Were it not for them, I never would have had the courage to take the plunge and write this book.

I first want to thank my incredible husband, Derrick, who has been my greatest supporter in this endeavor. Never once did he question my desire to write a book or the timing of it. He could not have been more of a rock for me to lean on during my great sorrow. When I needed someone to talk to, he listened. When I needed a shoulder to cry on, he was always there for me. He stood by me during my darkest days. He has been sensitive to my needs and ready to step in with the kids anytime I needed a break. He has patiently and willingly sacrificed many hours with me while I sat at the computer working on this book late into the night. He has prayed for me and with me when I didn't have the words to speak or strength to go on. I could never be the parent of five children had God not given me such a supportive and involved spouse to be my partner, advocate, and encourager.

I certainly could not have written this book without the inspiration of my five children, Carter, Reese, Sienna, Lawson, and Evangeline. You all helped me to keep smiling on even the toughest days. May you treasure these words as you grow older and remember the God of your youth. May you never stray far from Him and always look to Him for guidance and strength. I love each one of you with all of my heart.

I want to thank Mom and Dad for reading my writings for the past decade, for loving me unconditionally, and for being sources of encouragement for me. My mom has inspired me with her faith throughout my entire life. When I look at each of you, I see courage, faith, and determination. I dearly love you both!

To my dear friend Kaiya, who inspired me to start blogging 10 years ago, I will always be grateful. You have been my steadfast friend since we were young and are a great inspiration to me. I have watched you persevere through your own trials and suffering for many years and you are one of the strongest women I know.

I want to thank Aunt Carol and Aunt Pat for believing in me and praying for me steadfastly. You inspire me with your faith and perseverance and I am so thankful that you urged me to write this book.

I have many friends who are my prayer warriors. I turned to you in moments of doubt and difficulty and you lifted me up to the Lord. Your prayers were always felt! Thank you, Liz, Bethany, Kelly K., Kelly W., Ericka, and Emily for living out the truth found in James: "The earnest prayer of a righteous person has great power and produces wonderful results" (James 5:16 NLT).